Pride…The Root to Destruction

Pride...The Root to Destruction

Ronnie J. Wells

Writers Club Press
San Jose New York Lincoln Shanghai

Pride...The Root to Destruction

Writers Club Press
an imprint of iUniverse.com, Inc.

For information address:
iUniverse.com, Inc.
5220 S 16th, Ste. 200
Lincoln, NE 68512
www.iuniverse.com

ISBN: 0-595-18641-6

Printed in the United States of America

Dedication

First of all, I must acknowledge and give thanks to God – the Father, the Son, and the Holy Spirit. Without God, I can do nothing. I dedicate this book to my father, Johnny Wells, Sr. May you rest in peace. Thank you for making my life worth living. Even though we were raised in the projects without all of the necessities of life, you found a way to find joy and peace during the midst of our storms. Thank you for giving me the confidence to believe that God lives in me, which gave me the strength and the courage to make the best out of any situation in my life. I will never forget you and I will always cherish every moment we spent together. We had many days that we never spoke a word to each other. However, those were some of the best conversations that we ever had. Daddy (Jake Sr.) I LOVE YOU!

Your baby,
Ronnie (Jake Jr.) Wells

Contents

Foreword

Pride…the root to destruction is a book that will reveal the different ways an individual can commit this evil sin known as pride. Pride is an inward attitude that will lead a person into any outward known behavior: lust or confusion; arrogance or ignorance; or even laziness and procrastination. Pride has been labeled as one of the top 7 cardinal sins of the bible: the things that God despises the most (Proverbs 6:16-19). Pride will destroy a person from the inside out. Pride is mainly associated with 'inner-views'. This book will uncover the 'hidden' sins of the heart: sins that are omitted, unintentional or even thought about or spoken.

Pride…the root to destruction will also help an individual to realize the root or motive behind their personality and the reasons why they do the things that they do. It determines the reason why people act in certain ways, but most importantly, this book also gives practical solutions to overcoming pride. This book is spiritual based, with spiritual solutions since pride is a spiritual issue.

The bible declares that God wants to bless us and it also declares that the devil cannot stop us. Now, it seems that the only person who stands in our way is—"I". This book will help any person, who is willing to face reality and make a change in their lives, to understand that 'self' must be moved out of the way. Thus, we can now realize and believe that our true purpose in life can more readily be achieved, which is to fulfill God's will.

Through God's word, I want to uncover, reveal, expose and get rid of all the excuses and reasons used by people to justify why they have developed a certain type of personality and lifestyle. You will learn that your needs are only met by God. You will receive faith and belief that there is hope for everyone. Anyone can change, once the desire to change is present.

Pride...the root to destruction will help every individual to fulfill the will of God for their lives and it will also allow for the love of God to flow through them like rivers of living water. Open your hearts, your mind and your eyes to finally discover and release the 'real' you–your spirit who dwells within!

Acknowledgements

Special thanks to my wife Conchata Wells, who has been my power twin-patience. Thanks to my children for your obedience in letting me finish my 'homework': Jeremy and Zakarius; Camara and Breana; and little Ms. Ronni Christina. Thanks to my mother, Annie Wells; my brother and sister-in-law, David and Virginia; and my sisters, Ileane Wells and the late Christine Wells for all your spiritual support. Thanks to my mother-in-law Beretha Sanders for your love and concern. Thanks to all of my many nieces and nephews, close friends, relatives and everyone who has supported, prayed and interceded for me during my journey from pride to humility. Your prayers have availed much. Thanks to my 'best friends' who have always been there for me for over 20 years: Walter Brown, Vincent Sims, Tony Copeland, Charles Watkins and Sharon Cheeves. (You taught me well!) Thanks to my publisher, iUniverse, their staff and all personnel who have assisted me. Special acknowledgments to my local church, World Changers Church International for the word of God being taught by our pastors with simplicity and understanding. Thanks to the WCCI Barrier Breakers Men's Ministry and a special thanks to my spiritual father, Minister Danny Finkley and to Kelvin Nelson who both are my 5:00am daily prayer partners. This book represents my life that the Lord has directed me to place on these pages. May the spirit of the Lord come upon every believer that reads, understands and receives His word.

Introduction

(What is pride?....introduction)

Why is it the first of the seven cardinal sins that God despises (Proverbs 6:16-19)? Pride, for so long, has been related to arrogance. A prideful person was considered to be the type who "bragged" about himself. He was the type that could do no wrong. He received a lot of respect since so much time and efforts were put into his "accomplishments". When I played high school basketball our team chant was 'What's it all about? Pride!!!' Our coach wanted us to take our part of the team as being very important. He did not want us to take our skills or the game of basketball for granted. If only we knew what the driving force behind winning pride was back then, we probably would not have said what we said. The driving force behind pride was actually fear. It was fear of losing a basketball game.

Pride defined: 1. A sense of one's own proper value or dignity: self-respect, protecting one's image. 2. Pleasure or satisfaction taken in one's work, achievements or possessions: proud. When one's status or sense of self is measured. Proud of one's children. 3.a. A source of pride. 3.b. The most successful or thriving condition: prime. 4a. An overly high opinion of oneself: conceit. To esteem or indulge or submerge in self-esteem. 5. Haughty. 6. Properly valuing oneself, one's honor or one's dignity: too proud to accept charity. There are many forms and levels of pride. Pride can come in the most obvious ways or even in the most subtle and secretive way. Is it pride when a person doesn't ask for help?

Is it pride when they try to solve a problem on their own? Even though someone once said that experience is the best teacher, will asking for help stop him or her from growing in life? Ask yourself this question: Did God intend for His children to learn by their good experiences or by their bad experiences?

I want to show you why pride is the very first sin that God mentioned, which he totally despises. First of all, hard times do not always produce change in an individual. Change comes from within the heart and not from outside circumstances. If you place a poor man in a rich neighborhood, with the same poverty mentality and attitude, he'll more than likely become poor again. God uses love to teach people a lesson and not anger. A soft answer or a kind gesture will turn wrath and not arguing or fighting blow for blow or turning your back on people.

What does pride have to do with all this? Pride grieves the Holy Spirit. Pride hinders the flow of God's love. Pride is always in God's way. Pride places a person's attention on himself and not on God. When a person is walking in pride, he is not walking by faith. 'Whatsoever a person does that is not of faith is sin' (Romans 14:23). If pride is in the way whom will God show His grace and mercy to? If pride is in the way, how can God's covenant be established? God's covenant with Abraham is that we are blessed to be a blessing until all families of the earth have been blessed.

Pride will stop a person from giving or receiving a blessing. Pride is the #1 factor that can and will hinder the love of God. In order for the love of God to flow, pride must be out of the way so we can be in a position to receive. It is the dream of the Father to bless His children. God wants to restore unto us everything that the devil stole from us. The bible says that 'the earth is the Lord's and the fullness thereof' (Psalm 24:1). 'For all that is in the world, the lust of the flesh, and the lust of the eyes, and the pride of life, is not of the Father, but is of the world' (1John 2:16).

In this book you'll learn how to discern this evil spirit called pride. You'll learn how to cast this demon so you can begin to walk in peace and humility. In the book of Romans 12:3 'to every man that is among you, not to think more highly than he ought to think; but to think soberly, according as God hath dealt to every man the measure of faith'. God says not to have an exaggerated opinion of your own importance (Amplified). This opinion can be either good or bad. Do you feel like you are 'God's gift to the world' or do you wish you were never born? Either thought will be considered thinking more highly. Pride can exalt itself higher or lower than its situation or circumstance. When we think soberly, our mind is sound. Our mind is not drunken or confused with any outside substances or distractions. We should think according to the degree or measure of faith that God has given us. Pride thinks for itself. Now, you are probably beginning to see how pride is despised so much by God. It is very destructive. Pride is the root to destruction.

Chapter 1

The Road to Pride...lust

I once had a vision of a businessman sitting in a restaurant eating lunch. Only a few years later I had a vision of the same businessman, except, this time he was homeless. What happened in such a short amount of time? Well, when I saw him in the restaurant, the Lord revealed to me that he was thinking. "What should I do? Should I ask for help? Should I apply for a loan? If I asked for help would that mean I'm irresponsible? Would that mean I let myself down as well as my family? What would people think of me then? How would I look? I have an image I'm supposed to keep. I can't let people see me down like this. I can't let people see me asking for help. I really don't need any help. I can do this on my own. I didn't get this far being lazy. Besides, I've always taken care of myself. As a matter of fact, I've even taken care of a lot of other people, but every time I help someone they don't appreciate it."

"I'd rather just not bother with people. I don't need them anyhow. People don't love you anyway, so why should I love them? Yeah, all they will probably do is give me some advice. I don't need advice right now. I need solutions. I need money! I can get it on my own. I can't show any signs of weakness. I'm a strong man. A weak person would give in and ask for help. I'm not weak. I can never let them see me sweat. I don't sweat and furthermore, I don't like this feeling either. It's like going down a dark road and not knowing what is at the end or what the future will hold. It's scary at times because I'm too strong to fail. What if I fail and can't get up?"

"I wonder will the church help me get up. I attended church when I was young. Basically, I was in church all of my life. They will probably just tell me that I should not have made a mistake anyway. They will probably just tell me to pray. Well, next time I'll try something different. You never get a second chance to make a first impression. I have standards and I'm not accepting anything less. I'd rather sleep in the streets than to accept a lower paying job and end up in an apartment. I'm too good for that. I've come too far to go backwards."

"I have given to people all of my life and now look what has happened. I need some money and where is the help now? I've even given to the church. The preacher probably spent it on his car since he has been talking about tithing so much. That tithe was probably placed in his pocket. How can he get it to God? They say the more you give then the more you receive. Yeah, right! Next time, I will keep my little nest egg with me until I've saved and built up enough money to take care of myself. Just in case something like this happens again, I will have something to fall back on. I'll just take a little more time to think. The next business decision I make is going to be as good as gold before I invest anything."

"The next time, I won't ask anybody for advice. I am my own best judge. As a matter of fact, I just won't ask anybody for anything. I really don't need them anyway. My friends say to have patience. I don't have time to wait. If you snooze, you lose. Things need to start happening now! Well, I guess I'll go back to work. Better yet, why should I go back to work? I will pay myself more than anybody else will pay me. I'm worth a lot more than man can ever think of."

Have any of these thoughts reminded you of anyone? Have any of these thoughts ever crossed your mind? Did they remind you of yourself? There is one common factor in everything he said. PRIDE! Notice what is in the middle of the word pride—'I'. Pride is simply exalting oneself higher or lower than his situation or circumstance. Pride is like putting yourself before God. Pride is a form of fear. Pride is destructive. Pride is a spirit. In the story you just read this businessman operated totally in pride. Every thought he had was selfish. This selfishness is what took him from a successful businessman to a homeless man sleeping in the streets. It is not always necessary for a drastic event to take place such as death, financial problems, loss of employment or a life-threatening medical condition that will lead a person to destruction. 'The small foxes spoil the vine' (Song of Solomon 2:15).

So many times we make the mistake of comparing our lives to other people. According to us, nobody's situation is worse than ours. Remember that regardless of how bad you think your problem is, there is someone else who is probably far worse. We tend to approach a situation one-sided. When we do that, we enter into a form of pride called jealousy. Jealousy is when you want to have more or you want for someone else to have less than you do. Jealousy makes you feel as if you are missing out or losing something. 'God is a jealous God' (Exodus 20:5). This did not mean that He wants us to have less, but He wants us to recognize that without Him we don't exist. God's jealousy grew out of love for us and not for selfish motives. God's jealousy was to protect us and to provide for us. God knows what we've been through. He knows where we are today and what lies ahead of us tomorrow. Since He loves us so much and wants to care for His children and make sure that His children are safe, jealousy grew. Nobody will take care of us the way God will.

Now, as for mankind, his jealousy is for selfish reasons only. When people are always jealous, most times it is only a clear indication of what is missing from their own lives. It is a sign of insecurity within them. Jealousy can be selfish and it is, indeed, a form of pride. Jealousy is not concerned with how someone else would feel or if another individual is being blessed. In order for a jealous person to build himself up he chooses to try and tear someone else down. Pride tries to accomplish that very thing. Pride wants to exalt itself higher or lower in order to bring more attention to it. We should rejoice when we see other children of God being blessed. We should never look down on someone else unless we are looking down to bring him or her back up. In the beginning pride may appear that it is happy for you, but as time goes on, it grows its ugly head like the tares appear in the midst of the wheat.

Pride is lustful. Lust does not only pertain to sex but it is any desire outside of the will of God. We can lust for food, clothing, money, power, and prestige, attention and so much more. Lust can never be satisfied. It just wants more and more similar to a fireplace consuming wood. It will never get enough. A look will turn into lust just like a social drinker can turn into an alcoholic. Proudness can turn into arrogance. Being proud or excited about an achievement is a natural reaction. However, too much proudness is dangerous. Sugar is a very sweet and tasty substance, but taken in large quantities for a long period of time can make you sick.

We must be careful that our high esteem and appreciation for our accomplishments is not taken in large quantities. This is where being proud of an achievement turns into arrogance. We lose focus on how we got to where we are.

The Apostle Paul was a very confident man, but at the same time, he had balance. Contrary to popular belief, Paul did not walk in pride. In 2 Corinthians 12:6-7, the thorn in Paul's flesh was not an attempt by God to keep Paul humble. The devil, the messenger of Satan, was trying to make Paul exalt himself by using thorns. These thorns were people that tried to put pressure on Paul to try and make him conform to the world's standards. The thorns were placed in Paul's flesh to try to stop him from exalting God. He was giving God the glory for his existence. People thought Paul was bragging about himself, but he only wanted to brag about God's goodness, grace and mercy. Throughout the New Testament Paul acknowledged where his help came from. In Philippians 4:13 Paul said 'I can do all things through Christ which strengthened me'. His help came from Christ, the anointed one and His anointing. Paul recognized that without God he could do nothing but with God he could do anything.

Ask yourself: are you trying to impress God or are you trying to impress people? 'For all that is in the world, the lust of the flesh, and the lust of the eyes, and the pride of life, is not of the Father, but is of the world' (1 John 2:16). We should always be proud or joyful of our accomplishments, but we should also give God the glory for giving us the strength and the ability for our high achievements. In the book of Deuteronomy 8:17-18 'we should remember that it is God who giveth us power to get wealth that his covenant may be established'. We should be proud of ourselves because God has blessed us in order to bless someone else. It doesn't matter whether we bless them financially, materially, or spiritually. We can even bless them through encouragement by our testimonies. The testimony can help them get rid of their own failures and faults. Our achievements and blessings are not to bless us but they are to bless others.

Chapter 2

Protect My Image.......bondage

One area of pride that really hindered my personal growth was my image. All the way through high school I was an honor student and an honor graduate. I was voted most likely to succeed. Family, friends and even teachers looked up to me—Ronnie.

Ronnie Wells, Jake Wells' son from Carver Heights in Griffin, GA. They knew I was going to make it in life. Unfortunately, hanging around the wrong crowd, alcohol and irresponsibility sent my life on a roller coaster ride for 12 years. I still set goals and high achievements. I have always stayed employed. My addiction to alcohol along with my ability to keep a job classified me as a "functional" alcoholic. Even though the substance abuse problem is over, the "bad harvests" from all the "bad seed" that I sowed begin to manifest. The word of God makes it very clear that 'you will reap what you sowe' (Galatians 6:7). The word of God also says that 'as long as the earth remain seedtime and harvest shall not cease' (Genesis 8:22).

Money problems, bad credit, separation from my children, no furniture, no transportation and many other problems all followed me. The list can go on and on. Since my pride wanted to keep the "successful honor graduate image" from high school, I avoided going around certain people who knew me and what I used to be like. I wanted people to only remember "Jake Wells son", the star student from Griffin. I had no social life. I was ashamed of my apartment so I rarely entertained guests. When I would ride the bus to and from work, I would normally get off at an earlier bus stop. This way I could walk the back way into the building so too many people would not see me and ask questions as to why I was not driving.

As you can tell, I was trapped in people bondage. I was so concerned with my image and how I would look to people. PRIDE! Pride had me in bondage to myself and in bondage to the world. In Romans 12:2 'be not conformed to the world but to be transformed by renewing your mind'. I was conforming to the world and did not realize it. I was trying to impress the world and be what I thought they wanted to see. Christians should not want to be like the world but the world should want to be like us. We are made in the image of God so the only image we should be concerned about is God. How does God see us? How do we look, talk or act in the eyes of God? We should be concerned with impressing the One that made us and who protects us, and not the one that is against us.

Now, keep in mind that we should set standards for our personal appearance. After all, we are representing our heavenly Father. In 1 Thessalonians 5:22 God said to 'abstain from all appearances of sin'. However, we don't need to talk, walk, act or look like a sinner in any area of our lives. We don't even need to go out in public in a way that is not presentable to God. It won't hurt to exert a little more effort in the way that we dress. We should do like Romans 12:1 and 'present our bodies a living sacrifice, holy, acceptable unto God'.

My conforming to the world began early. It began with peer pressure. In the book of Proverbs 7:6-27 is the story of the harlot's house. It speaks of a young man, surrounded by peers, who basically felt out of place. King Solomon observed this young man from his window in which he called these youths "simple" or void of understanding. Naive is a good way to describe them. Well, this young man apparently wanted to prove something to himself. He would walk by this woman's house, in which she was very physically attractive, just to look inside her window. He appeared to be somewhat of a "peeping Tom". One day, she waited outside for him to pass by. She caught him, kissed him and eventually seduced him. What has this story to do with pride? Pride was the initial driving force that led him to walk by this harlot's house. His bondage to people, in trying to keep and protect his "lover-boy" image, led him into a destructive situation. If the young man had asked God to direct his paths instead of being driven by this desire to protect his image, this entire adulterous situation would have been avoided.

I once heard someone say that image meant nothing to them. Now I understand what they meant. We must put more focus on our needs first. Drop your image. Drop your pride and thirst for Jesus Christ, the anointed one and His anointing. The bible says that 'the things which are seen are temporary (subject to change) but the things which are not seen are eternal' (2 Corinthians 4:18). If you don't like your bad image or if you have a low self-esteem, just remember that what you see is only temporary. It can and will change as long as you want it to change. Beauty is in the eye of the beholder. Beauty is always in a person's heart and not only from a physical, outside appearance. This is what God looks at—your heart, your spirit. If you think you can change or if you think that you can't change, then guess what-you're probably right! On the other hand, if you are overly concerned with protecting your good image, it too is subject to change. An image, good or bad is only temporary, however, God's love, grace and mercy is eternal.

Have you ever wondered where these images come from or what exactly is an image? Thoughts that are gathered together are what form an image. Before God had an image, He had to think it first. God had an idea or a blueprint of how man would look. His imagination was at work. Once He had the image, the next thing He did was to create it. How did God create man? Man was created with words. In Genesis 1 God created everything once He "said" what He was imagining. The words produced the manifestation. Once God said 'let us make man in our image', man was made immediately. If you don't like your image then don't speak it. Your words are like spiritual containers that hold the material to bring your thoughts and images into existence. The only image we should be concerned about is the one that is in line and in agreement to the word of God.

What about my reputation? Well, let me tell you like this. Jesus said that I don't have a reputation (Philippians 2:7). The world's system will place a reputation on you based on what they see. Their opinions originate from thoughts that they have gathered. These thoughts form an image or an impression. Once this image is spoken from their mouth and planted in their hearts, a reputation is manifested. The reputation is their confirmation of the thought, image or impression they had of you. This reputation is based only on what they see. Reputations and images can change. This is why people can have a good or bad reputation. They change because the flesh will change. Remember that the things that are seen are temporary.

Now, why did Jesus say He was of no reputation? Jesus did not have a reputation because He never changed. He could not change. Why? Think about how Jesus came to this earth. 'In the beginning was the Word, and the Word was with God, and the word was God' (John 1:1). 'And the Word was made flesh, and dwelt among us, (and we beheld his glory, the glory as the only begotten of the Father) full of grace and truth' (John 1:14). Jesus was actually God in the flesh.

God cannot and will not change. The trinity order is that we are spirit beings, we possess a soul or mind and we live in a physical body. People were trying to place a reputation on Jesus when in actuality they could not see Him. They did not see His spirit therefore there was no real means to give Him any type of reputation. Since we are spirit beings, our "reputation" in the eyes of the world does not matter at all.

God is a spirit and we are made in the image of God. God sees our spirit. God talks to us through our spirit. The bible says that 'the spirit of a man is the candle of the Lord' (Proverbs 20:27). This means that God communicates and searches our inner man through our spirit. We should only be concerned about our spirit man. Is it clean? Is it right with God? Has it been renewed? It is a chain reaction.

The spirit controls the mind and the mind controls the body. If your spirit is in line with the word of God then your flesh will too. Stop trying to protect your image. We must protect our spirit. The bible says to 'guard your heart (spirit) for out of it are the issues of life' (Proverbs 4:23). The image the world sees is not the real you. The spirit man is the real you. Everything that is associated with your life comes out of your spirit. Reputations and images only see the flesh, however God's reputation and image of you is in the spirit. In Mark 7:20-23 'And he said, That which cometh out of the man, that defileth the man. For from within, out of the heart of men, proceed evil thoughts, adulteries, fornications, murders, Thefts, covetousness, wickedness, deceit, lasciviousness, an evil eye, blasphemy, pride, foolishness: All these things come from within, and defile the man'.

What can you do about the thoughts that we gather on our own that produce this image? Well, we can simply change the way we think and the things that we think about. In Philippians 4:8-9 'Finally, brethren, whatsoever things are true, whatsoever things are honest, whatsoever things are just, whatsoever things are pure, whatsoever things are lovely, whatsoever things are of good report: if there be any virtue, and if there be any praise, think on these things. Those things, which ye have both learned, and received, and heard, and seen in me, do: and the God of peace shall be with you'. God wants to take into consideration and have an account of those things we can give praise for. We should allow the blessings that we have received be on our minds. In the Amplified bible, verse 9 'practice what you have learned and received and heard and seen in me, and model your way of living on it, and the God of peace (of untroubled, undisturbed well-being) will be with you'. We should pattern our ways and lifestyle after God. He is the God of peace. We need to set our affections on Him.

If these thoughts and imaginations continue to form in your mind, look at 2 Corinthians 10:4-5 '(For the weapons of our warfare are not carnal, but mighty through God to the pulling down of strongholds;) Casting down imaginations, and every high thing that exalteth itself against the knowledge of God, and bringing into captivity every thought to the obedience of Christ'. We must pull down strongholds.

What are strongholds? They are thoughts that have a strong hold of your mind. These strongholds produce images. God wants us to cast down any thought or imagination that does not agree with the knowledge of God. These thoughts and imaginations must then be brought into captivity. We must capture these thoughts. We must lock these thoughts up until they obey Christ. These thoughts must agree with Christ. Do not let your thoughts run loose, but capture them.

Let your thought know that it must be in agreement with Christ. How do you let that thought know? You must speak to it. You must confess the word of God so that the thought will know how to obey Christ. We capture thoughts by speaking the word of God. Really? Yes. In order to be born again, you must do two things according to Romans 10:9-10. We must believe in our heart and confess with our mouth that Jesus was raised from the dead for our sins. The confession is what makes our salvation established. The confession confirms our belief. So likewise, when you confess a thought, this means you believe in what you are thinking. If you do not believe in a thought, do not confess it.

In Matthew 6:31 'therefore take no thought, saying, What shall we eat? or, What shall we drink? Or, Wherewithal shall we be clothed'? This scripture is saying that even though you have a lot of problems that you are thinking about; do not take those thoughts by saying them. Don't confess those thoughts. Don't take that thought. If you do not want it, do not take it by saying it. Don't worry about the thoughts of tomorrow because tomorrow will take care of itself. In Matthew 6:34 'take therefore no thought for the morrow: for the morrow shall take thought for the things of itself. Sufficient unto the day is the evil thereof'. 'Tomorrow will have worries and problems of its own' (amplified).

If you let that thought remain, it will produce a stronghold or an image in your mind. Instead of allowing that thought to stay in your mind, we must capture it. Once the thought is captured, it must be brought into the obedience of Christ. In order to bring a thought to Christ, we must confess the word of God. This is why it so important to protect our image. Not the image of the world, but the image of Christ.

Chapter 3

Condemnation-I shouldn't make mistakes...incomplete

Pride leads to condemnation. Condemnation is an incomplete or empty emotion felt when a person makes a mistake. It is guilt that sets in the heart that makes a person feels like they are not worthy of God's love because of their actions. Condemnation blocks the flow of the anointing in your life just like a dam blocks the flow of water in a river. People tend to set high standards or resolutions for their lives, but if their goal is not reached, the guilt will set in; basically causing them to 'condemn' their own lives. This leads to not feeling worthy or righteous. However, according to 2 Corinthians 5:21 'Jesus, who knew no sin, was made sin that we may be made the righteousness of God'. So, instead of waddling in our sins, we should pick ourselves up, dust ourselves off and start over again.

We are righteous, because of the blood of Jesus, regardless of how we feel. Righteousness is a gift. There is nothing you can do to earn a gift. The gift of righteousness is yours to keep, regardless of how you feel or regardless of what you do. Once you get born again and confess that Jesus Christ died and rose from the dead for your sins, you receive this gift.

God gave a commandment in Job 40:6-7, when he appeared out of a whirlwind and said to Job: 'gird up thy loins now like a man. I will demand of thee and declare thou unto me'. He literally told Job to pull up his pants, stop feeling sorry for himself, and to declare his rights from God by accepting his gift of righteousness. Stop worrying about the mistakes, but focus on the solution. 'Not a novice, lest being lifted up with pride he fall into condemnation of the devil' (1 Timothy 3:6). Also, in Isaiah 43:25-26 God said 'I, even I am He that blotteth out thy transgressions for mine own sake, and will not remember thy sins. Put me in remembrance: let us plead together, declare thou that thou may be justified'. Again we see God telling us to get your attention off of the problem. God said He is not the one who is remembering our sins. We are. In 1 John 1:9 'if we confess our sins, He is faithful and just to forgive us our sins and to cleanse us from all unrighteousness'.

Now, what have these examples to do with pride? First of all, as long as we are on this earth we will never be 'perfect' based on the world's definition. The world's definition of being perfect is 110% without fault. To be perfect in the eyes of God means to be complete or whole in Christ. We will be complete once we are in heaven. In 2 Timothy 4:7 Paul said 'I have fought a good fight, I have finished my course, I have kept the faith'. His striving for perfection was centered on the word of God. The fulfillment of what God has in store for us lies in heavenly places.

The earth is full of sin, chaos and filthiness. When I think about the earth, it reminds me of how dust falls from the atmosphere and builds up on your furniture. We don't see the dust falling, but once we wipe the furniture, all of the dirt will appear. In the natural, we need to take a bath every day. Even though we may not have done things throughout the day that will show the obvious reasons to why our bodies are dirty, dust is still falling from the sky. This is why dirt is on us. There is no dirt in heaven. There is no sin in heaven. We will be clean every day. The earth we live on today is full of sin.

In Psalm 51:10 David said to God: 'create in me a clean heart, O God: and renew the right spirit within me'. One reason David asked for a clean heart and a renewed spirit was because of sin that is already in the earth. He recognized that the only requirement to being a sinner was to be born (Psalm 51:5). This is why perfection is not on the earth. There is too much sin on this earth. 'We live in this world, but we are not of this world' (John 15:19). Once Jesus comes back to take us to heaven to be with the Father, it will be at that point that we will have reached completeness. Jesus died on the cross that we might have life. He was made sin for us in order to make us righteous: in order to give us rights during our stay here.

Pride fools you into thinking that you should be perfect on this earth. You can't. Personally, I thought I was perfect. I worked for the local Telephone Company making a nice amount of money. I drove a nice car, lived in a very nice and decent apartment and had a generous bank account. There were so many material things in place in my life until I felt content and complete. However, there was no peace in my spirit. I always felt there was something missing in life. It wasn't until I rededicated my life to Jesus Christ that I found the missing link. My spirit was grieved. I grew up in church and I have always been taught Christian values. Even though my flesh was being satisfied, which made me "feel" complete, my spirit was starving and incomplete.

Remember that we live in a world of sin that falls on this earth just as if dust is falling to the ground. Therefore, even though a person may feel as if they were clean or perfect yesterday, today is totally new. As Christians we are encouraged to take a spiritual bath everyday. We bathe in the word of God. People who feel that they should not make mistakes is actually making mistakes-whether mistakes are intentional or not. We must take a 'spiritual bath' every day. If not, we have already failed our complete and perfect status. A humble Christian is more perfect than a person who walks in pride. The Christian is renewing his mind, asking God for a clean heart and praying for the right spirit. If your spirit is not new, then it is old. Anything that is old, used, or tarnished is not perfect. Is God cleaning you?

Nobody likes to fail. I don't. I'm striving for perfection; however, my motivation is to be like Christ. The Apostle Paul was striving for perfection. He said in Philippians 3:12-14 'that even though I have not apprehended or grasped a complete hold of perfection, there is one thing that I do. I forget those things that are behind and reach forth unto things which are before. I press toward the mark for the prize of the high calling of God in Christ Jesus'. Paul was pressing towards God. My mistake in the past was striving for things that are on this earth. Perfection is not on this earth. Perfection is in God through Jesus Christ. 'Jesus is the manifested word of God' (John 1:1, 14). Therefore, perfection is in God's word.

God is complete. God is perfect. We should learn from Paul and press for the prize. The prize he was striving for will not collect dust. The prize he was striving for will not change. The prize he was striving for was anointed. This prize removed burdens and destroyed yokes. This prize was eternal life and joy. The prize was the anointing. If you are striving for earthly perfection then ask yourself, what is the prize? What is the reward? Who will present this prize? How long will these earthly prizes last? I have realized that prizes on this earth are only temporary, but my heavenly prizes are eternal. Do not condemn yourself for mistakes you make on this earth. We should repent, ask God for forgiveness and move on with our lives.

Unless Jesus Christ is the head of your life; unless you are a born again Christian; unless you walk by faith and the word of God, then there is no such thing as true perfection. Bible perfection is not based on the world's standards but on God's standards. What I have learned as a man of God is that even though I'm striving to be perfect in the eyes of God, I realize that I am not there yet. This will not happen until I reach heaven.

I don't teach my children to be perfect based on the world's system, but I teach them how to deal with and change the imperfections of their own lives. Do not focus on everything that is only right, but also correct areas in your life that needs improvement. There is a phrase that says "if it's not broke, don't fix it". Even if it's not broke there is always room for improvement. There is always another level to grow. We should pray everyday for forgiveness of sins committed and omitted.

There are things we do that we know are wrong, but what about the ones that are not so obvious. What about anger, holding grudges, unforgiveness, jealousy or those inward, emotional sins? If this type of sin is in your life then you still have not reached perfection. You are still making mistakes. These omitted sins should be dealt with.

In my spirit, true perfection and a mistake free life are on the inside of a person. Once you can say that you are not making any mistakes both inside and outside of your body, at that time you can say you have reached perfection. Since our spirit is who we are and not our flesh, then we must be in a place where our flesh won't be an issue or a hindrance. The only place that I can see that taking place is in heaven with our Father.

Make sure that you are confessing, reading and meditating on the word of God everyday. 'The thief cometh to kill, steal and to destroy but

Jesus came so we would have life and have it more abundantly' (John 10:10). 'Seek ye first, the kingdom of God and all things shall be added unto you' (Matthew 6:33).

A true example of a man striving for perfection in God can be seen in King David. In Acts 13:22 God said 'I have found David the son of Jesse, a man after mine own heart, which shall fulfill all my will'. What a statement! David? He was the same murderer that killed King Uriah because David committed adultery with this king's wife, Bathsheba causing her to become pregnant (2Samuel 11:1-27). David? The man who constantly fornicated until he contracted all types of venereal diseases (Psalm 38:1-22).

Yes, David was a man after God's own heart, in spite of his mistakes. How, you ask? In Psalm 51:1-19 David poured his heart and soul out before God. He did this regardless of what people thought about him. He acknowledged his faults and only wanted to be justified in the eyes of God (Verses 3-4). He wanted a clean heart, a renewed spirit and for the joy of the Lord to be restored unto him (verses 10-13).

This king was not too 'prideful' to repent and ask for forgiveness. He had a complete change of mind, a change of heart and a change of his direction. David was tired of sin and pride. David had enough of evilness. Even in Psalm 38 David went before God, dropped all forms of pride and begged God for forgiveness. He wanted God to hear his voice and for God to still be with him (verses 15-22).

Now, what type of 'king' are you? Do you think you will never make a mistake in your life? Do you think you are perfect? Once God saw David's earnest, sincere and heartfelt desire to turn away from sin and to turn towards God, He knew David was now equipped to be the man after His own heart. In Psalm 89:20, the Lord found David, received him and anointed him with the burden removing, yoke destroying power of God-the anointing.

Pride is a burden. Pride tries to make you exalt yourself up high to a point where you think that you are faultless. Pride will make you think that you should be perfect and that you should not make any mistakes. Once you make a mistake, then the spirit of guilt and condemnation will set in. Do not allow pride to pick you up and drop you back down. You need to drop pride and all of its faults and mistakes. Protect yourself by 'putting on the whole armour of God that you will be able to stand up against all the strategies, tricks and deceitfulness of the devil' (Ephesians 6:11). Your armour is the anointing!

The anointing can remove any type of burden. It does not matter what type of burden you are faced with, it can and will be removed. The anointing is power. David endured a very difficult situation; however, he was able to overcome it. Although God showed up in his life, I also recognized what David was able to accomplish by obeying God. In 1 Samuel 30:6 'and David was greatly distressed; for the people spake of stoning him, because the soul of all the people was grieved, every man for his sons and for his daughters: but David encouraged himself in the Lord his God'. David encouraged himself because he knew his strength came from God. Although David had sinned, this did not stop him from having faith and trust in the power of God.

Always remember that even if you do not feel like forgiving yourself, God will. There is no limit as to how much God loves you. God does not want to see his children miserable or depressed. God wants us to be full of joy. We have joy in our spirit. If the joy is not there, then do not blame God. We are the ones that block up what God has placed in our spirit. We have been given the ability to put happiness back into our lives. This ability was demonstrated by David in 1 Samuel 30:6. The Amplified version says that David strengthened himself.

Do not allow a mistake to place your focus on the problem. We must simply repent, ask God for forgiveness, judge ourselves accordingly and move on with our lives. When we allow condemnation to dictate our lives, it will cause us to exist in this world. We must start back living our lives to the fullest. Be blessed with peace and increase!

Chapter 4

Need help? Ask, seek, knock...irresponsible

The key scripture to this book is Proverbs 16:18 which states that 'pride goes before destruction'. There have been many times when we may see a bad event happening to someone. We may have seen people in some sort of trouble. We may see a homeless person on the street, and our heart will go out to them. We try to help, but guess what? The help was refused. So many times help is offered to an individual, but because of pride, the help is not received. It is at this beginning stage when people refuse help that the destruction will come. Some people think that the destruction always happen first and a person's pride would not let them ask for assistance. The Lord revealed to me that pride was there first.

Let me share this story with you. I once met a young woman who was being evicted from her apartment. She would not ask family, friends, a shelter or the church for any help. She even refused assistance from me. She said: "I don't want people to know that I failed". "I let so many people down". "This is not the first time I lost an apartment". Once she was evicted from her apartment, she then chose to sleep on the street. She was living from place to place and basically anywhere. I was in contact with several resources that were willing and able to provide food, clothing and shelter for her. I tried continually to help, however, she kept moving so it was almost impossible to keep up with her. Once I did get in touch with her, all she would say was "God will deliver me".

At this point my friend begins to say she is walking by faith. God did promise in 1 Corinthians 10:13 that 'he will not allow you to be tempted or suffer more than you can handle, and would make a way to escape'. The way to escape being on the streets and being homeless was there for this lady. If she had obeyed the word of God in Matthew 7:7-8 '(Ask, and it shall be given you; seek, and ye shall find, knock and it shall be opened unto you:)' then she could have avoided sleeping on the streets. 'When pride cometh, then cometh shame: but with the lowly is wisdom' (Proverbs 11:2).

Now, many of you are saying 'just because she did not ask for help does not mean it was because of her pride. Maybe she wanted to make it on her own'. This is exactly my point. Pride puts the focus on the individual. Pride is concerned about "me, my and I". "This is 'my' problem or 'I' don't need anybody's help. Pride wants a person to keep their mouth shut and not ask for anything. While your mouth is shut, you limit God's ability to show you his grace and mercy towards you. How? 'Angels hearken to the voice of the word of God' (Psalm 103:20). The word of God on your voice is what calls the angels forth. God's word is producing the manifestation.

God wants to use His love to teach us—not hard times, pain, trouble or sleeping on the streets. In this case, this woman's pride was there first and then the destruction came. Once she was in the middle of her destruction, her testimony changed from "I don't need any help" to "I have faith in God". Faith should not be developed in the middle of a destructive situation. You should have faith before the destruction comes so it will not come near you. We have to be careful not to tempt God. We cannot jump off a bridge and then have faith that the angels of God will bear us up. We must have faith 'before' the fall; otherwise, the law of gravity will work, for what goes up must come down. The law of seedtime and harvest will operate. In Galatians 6:7 'be not deceived; God is not mocked: for whatsoever a man soweth, that shall he also reap'. It would have been faith for this woman if she had asked, seeked or knocked before the destruction. Faith is when you believe God right now that someone will bless you or a way will be provided. Her faith was the same as that person jumping off the bridge.

We hear testimonies all the time about trouble and turmoil in a person's life. However, how that situation originated is not always mentioned. Many times, pride was the destructive force from day one. A lot of temptation that we endure is self-inflicted. Christians are so quick to say that God is taking them through something to teach them a lesson or to help them grow up and mature. This is an easy way out of accepting responsibility for their actions, mistakes and failures. If we look in the mirror long enough, most of the time we are the one's taking ourselves through temptation, tests or trials—not God.

I remember hearing a story about a man whose boat overturned while on a fishing trip. He was about to drown. Three boats passed him while he was in the sea. They each offered to save him and to ask if he needed help. Each time he said 'no' because he was waiting for God. This man eventually drowned and died. When he got to heaven, he asked God, "Why didn't you save me"? God replied, "I sent 3 boats by to rescue you. What else did you want me to do"?

Do not confuse the favor of God with anything else. We must be careful not to miss the 'supernatural' blessings of God while waiting for a 'spectacular' event. So many times we miss God because we expect Him to show up on a 'cloud'. We look for God in all of the marvelous way. We expect for a one billion-dollar check to be in the mailbox. Some play the lottery or try a get rich quick type of method. We look for an angel to appear in the midst of our situation to offer us a handout. We should not limit the way God can bless us. God has millions of ways to provide for our needs, but all we need is one of them. God is a God who is always on time. He may not come when you want Him to come, but He will always be there right when you need him.

This is our problem. We expect God to show up when we want Him to come and how we want Him to come, instead of having faith and patience that He will. In

I John 5:14-15 'And this is the confidence that we have in Him, that, if we ask any thing according to His will, He heareth us: And if we know that He hear us, whatsoever we ask, we know that we have the petitions that we desired of Him'. If we don't ask, how can He hear us, and if God does not hear us then how will we have what we asked for? We will have what we ask when we ask in faith. Faith is not only knowing that God can but also knowing that God will. If you know that God will, the question of 'when' will not be an issue. It does not matter when God will bless you, but knowing God will bless you should be sufficient enough.

Let's go to the bible and read stories of people dropping pride and asking God for help. In Mark 5:25-34 there was a woman that had an issue of blood for twelve years. She had suffered a lot of pain trying to be healed by doctors and ending up spending all the money she had. This sounds like a case of someone with pride that chose to handle his or her own situation instead of asking God. However, when she heard about Jesus all of her pride was dropped. This woman pressed through a crowd of people in her sick condition. I can imagine how she looked after bleeding for twelve years. At this point she didn't care about looks, but all she knew was that

Jesus was available to heal her. The bible said she touched the hem of Jesus' garment and immediately virtue or manifested healing power left His body, came upon her and she was healed at that very moment.

How many of you will come before God on 'bended-knee' looking your worst? How many of you will be willing to humiliate yourself before men just to get to God? This woman did not care how she looked, how she felt, what she had on, or the money that she did not have. She did not care what people would think, what they would say, how they would look at her or how they would judge her. All that she cared about was Jesus was available to heal her.

In Mark 10:46-52 there was a blind man named Bartimaeus who sat by the highway side begging. He was going through extreme emotional and mental anguish because he was blind and wanted to see. He heard that Jesus was near him, which made him cry and scream for Jesus. He called for Jesus as loud as he could and did not care how it sounded or what people would think. A lot of people were trying to make him keep quiet, but instead he screamed even louder than before. "JESUS! HAVE MERCY ON ME"! Bartimaeus was desperate. He knew that Jesus was able to heal and there was no way in heaven that he was going to miss out on an opportunity like this.

Can you imagine if Jesus showed up and was standing right in front of you with everything that you need? Would you sit back and wait for Jesus to come to you or would you be like Bartimaeus and call on His name? JESUS!!! Bartimaeus did not have time for pride. He did not have time to sit back and wait to see what would happen next. His spirit was in high expectation and nothing in this physical or natural world could hold him back. He needed help so he asked for help. Jesus heard his cry. He called Bartimaeus forward and asked him 'What wilt thou that I should do unto thee'?

I believe Jesus hears our cry and has asked us "what do we want". Before Bartimaeus answered Jesus, he did something that was very interesting. In verse 50 it says that 'he, casting away his garment, rose, and came to Jesus'. Wearing the garment during his time symbolized that he was blind. A blind man today wears dark glasses and carries a walking stick to indicate their blindness. When he cast away his garment, it literally meant that Bartimaeus was taking off the thing that called him blind.

In other words, he was saying I believe that I can already see even before the manifestation had taken place. Since the garment meant he was blind, not wearing the garment meant he could see. Once he took off the garment, he rose and came to Jesus. In the Greek, one definition of the word rose is a repetition; intense reversal; upright and active. Bartimaeus was in high expectation. He was prepared even before Jesus came. He decided to change his position, leave his sorrow and depressed state behind him and seek to change his position in life.

Many times we try to handle problems on our own. However, when we seek God first, He will lead us and guide us in the direction He would have us to go in. We should not be so quick to refuse help. The bible says that we are blessed to be a blessing. God will work through someone else to bless you. By refusing help you could literally be refusing God. God wants to give us sweatless victory. God wants us to be more than conquerors. It does not matter how high or high low your status is in society, you cannot make it in this world without God.

In Luke 7:1-10 a centurion soldier, with a high ranking authoritative position in the army, dropped his pride and asked Jesus to heal one of his servants. This soldier' faith was a little different than the faith of Bartimaeus. Jesus said that this man had 'great faith' (verse 9). Why? Look at verses 6-7 and see what happened when Jesus was on his way to the soldier's home. 'Then Jesus went with them, And when He was now not far from the house, the centurion sent friends to him, saying unto him, Lord, trouble not thyself: for I am not worthy that shouldest enter under my roof: Wherefore neither thought I myself worthy to come unto thee: but say in a word, and my servant shall be healed'.

The soldier said it was not even necessary for Jesus to be present physically in his home. He had faith in the word of God. He knew that the word would heal his servant. He recognized the power that was in the word. Looking for a person to deliver them, to a point, can distract so many people that they forget about the power. They forget about the anointing of God. We need to put our focus more on the word of God and not always on the person speaking the word.

Personally, it was difficult for me to ask someone for help. Sometimes I chose to walk to work instead of asking someone for a ride. I would let my stomach growl like a lion from being hungry instead of asking for a meal. I also let my home utilities become disconnected instead of asking for a loan. I was in pride extremely bad. I thank God that I am free from that bondage. Since God has blessed me, I now look for opportunities to be a blessing. I am very sensitive to my spirit.

My spirit discerns when someone is in need. He let's me know when they are walking in pride. Based on my own testimonies and experiences, I now can minister to people in a way that will allow them to let one of God's servants become a blessing in their lives. 'Let us therefore come boldly unto the throne of grace, that we may obtain mercy, and find grace to help in time of need' (Hebrews 4:16).

Chapter 5

Pride to humility....guilt

Many people have a problem with the word humble. They see humility as a weakness. A humble person appears to be the one that will always turn the other cheek, be ridiculed, taken for granted or be used and abused. The word humble has sometimes been associated with loss or decrease because it may seem as if they are receiving the 'short end of the stick'. However, there is a balance to humility. In the world's system, people who accept less than his or her standards, in order for someone else to benefit, is considered weak. This world's system is selfish and is only concerned about increasing its life. It wants to hold the next person down in order for it to stay on top. Its attitude is 'I got mine-you get yours'. Being a blessing is very difficult to do because of pride. As you know, pride is concerned about "I".

Now, in the eyes of God, a strong person is the type who accepts less than their standards, in order for someone else to benefit. This is a strength that Christians need to learn how to do on a more consistent basis. We are blessed to be a blessing to someone else. The anointing on a person's life was not designed for that individual, but he is anointed to remove a burden from another person's life. In Ephesians 4:11-13 'and he gave some apostles; and some, prophets; and some, evangelists; and some, pastors and teachers; for the perfecting of the saints, for the work of the ministry, for the edifying of the body of Christ: Till we all come in the unity of the faith, and of the knowledge of the Son of God, unto a perfect man, unto the measure of the stature of the fullness of Christ'.

As you can see, God gave instructions that we build up the body of Christ until we all walk in unity, as one, in the fullness of Christ, the anointed one and His anointing. Once we recognize that we are on this earth to bless another person, our spirit will become more humble and we can walk and operate in true humility. Children of the world's system have a hard time being humble. They do not see themselves blessing another individual. They only see themselves losing more than they are gaining. A prideful person is not thinking about what they can give but rather on what they can get.

Being humble requires submission to God's will and then submission to others. This is how we honor God. We give Him complete and total dominion over our lives. We honor God when we let God's will be done. Thy kingdom come and Thine will be done. It's not about our will or our desires, but what will God want me to do.

Remember that humility has two parts; you are receiving less in order to bless someone else with more than they had before. It is NOT humility if people accept less to fulfill their own needs. It is NOT humility to move from a 5-bedroom home into a 2-bedroom apartment in order to save money. This is a wise, financial, business decision and just good common sense. However, if you know about a family with 10 members that live in a 2-bedroom apartment, a humble spirit will want to help. If your family has 5 members and live in a 5-bedroom home, you will gladly move in order to bless the other family.

Humility is an act of the heart and not of your emotions or actions. How can you tell if pride is in the way? You can tell if your motives are to benefit yourself alone. If you are acting out from your heart to help another person, you are then walking in humility. One vital test to distinguish the difference between pride and humility is based on who are you trying to exalt. Are you exalting yourself or God? When your motive is to exalt 'self', this is pride; however when your motive is to exalt God, this is humility.

It is dangerous to not walk in humility. Why? Because we are made in the image of God. Do you know what your spirit is made of? Do you know what is contained in the spirit? Do you know what comes out of your spirit? In Galatians 5:22-23 'but the fruit of the spirit is love, joy, peace, longsuffering, gentleness, goodness, faith, meekness (humility), temperance: against such there is no law'. There is no law because the fruit of the spirit is like a final decision-maker. Nothing can replace it or come against it. It will always stand. This fruit should always come forth out of our spirit. This is how we are to live our lives everyday. The bible tells us that 'a tree is known by its fruit' (Luke 6:44). Humility should flow out of your spirit. When we do not walk in the fruit of the spirit then we are actually walking against God and against His ordinances because the spirit is who God is.

How do you know when you are not walking in the fruit of the spirit? One way is a guilty conscious. If the fruit of the spirit is not flowing, then your spirit will become grieved and a guilty conscious will begin. Guilt is when you feel bad or uneasy because of something you said or did. Guilt will occur because your flesh is fighting against the spirit. This is what 'moves' our conscious. Our conscious is the balance between our spirit and our flesh. Our conscious is like an alarm clock that will alert you when you are not walking in the fruit of the spirit.

The fruit of the spirit, which by God's law, is suppose to produce love, joy, meekness, etc. I could not get rid of the guilt in my life until I got rid of pride. Pride stopped my spirit from flowing the way that God had intended. God is a spirit and the fruit of the spirit is what flows from Him.

What is our reward for being humble? In Matthew 5:3 Jesus said 'Blessed are the poor in spirit; for theirs is the kingdom of heaven'. In the amplified version it reads 'Blessed (happy, to be envied, and spiritually prosperous-with life-joy and satisfaction in God's favor and salvation, regardless of their outward conditions) are the poor in spirit (the humble, who rate themselves insignificant), for theirs is the kingdom of heaven'! Jesus said we would be blessed or spiritually prosperous with life.

Another definition of the word blessed is to be empowered to prosper. This just lets me know that when I do what God has instructed me to do, in this area of humility, He will reward me. He will bless me. I do not have to worry about decrease in my life when I am increasing someone else's life. It is a cycle. God will make sure that as long as you are being humble and blessing His children. He will make sure that you are prosperous. He will make sure that you remain blessed because He knows that you will bless someone else. He knows that you are 'a yielded vessel unto God and meet for the master's use' (2 Timothy 2:21).

Can God use you? Are you willing to yield yourself to God and allow His mercy to flow through you? Consider yourself as a "water hose" for Christ. In John 7:38 Jesus said 'He that believeth on me, as the scripture hath said, out of his belly shall flow rivers of living water'. Let the love of God flow. Let humility flow like a river. Some may think that they may have been humble or they may have helped people all of their lives and now it is time to reap what they have sown. It is time for somebody to show humility towards them. Fret not.

In 1 Peter 5:5 'Likewise, ye younger, submit yourselves unto the elder. Yea, all of you be subject one to another, and be clothed with humility: for God resisteth the proud, and giveth grace to the humble'. Also in Matthew 18:4 'Whosoever therefore shall humble himself as this little child, the same is greatest in the kingdom of heaven'. This just lets me know that God has not forgotten about any act of humility you have done. Now, what about the ones that are still 'hard-headed'? In James 4:6 'but he (God) giveth more grace. Wherefore he saith, God resisteth the proud, but giveth grace unto the humble'.

A person who walks in pride is a resistance to God. This resistance blocks up the flow of God's grace and mercy. The bible makes it very clear in determining whether or not a person is a true follower of Christ. In Matthew 12:30 Jesus said 'He that is not with me is against me; and he that gathereth not with me scattereth abroad'. Therefore, if you are not flowing with God then you are automatically flowing against him. If you are not going forward then you are going backwards.

God can flow through the humble. The humble have no barriers set up or limits established. The humble always let the will of God be done. The humble simply let God be God in their lives. People who walk in pride are actually setting themselves up for destruction. In Matthew 23:12 'And whosoever shall exalt himself shall be abased (humbled or brought low); and he that shall humble himself shall be exalted (raised to honor)'. So it appears, in the eyes of God, that when you exalt yourself up high, you are actually bringing yourself low. When you humble yourself you are raising yourself up.

Don't be deceived into thinking that being humble is being weak. Humility is actually strength. In the name of Jesus, I bind the spirit of pride and I declare that you have a humble spirit. Come out from among the prideful. In Proverbs 16:19 'it is better to be of an humble spirit with the lowly, than to divide the spoil with the proud'. Don't worry about what people think. In Psalm 37:1-3 'fret not thyself because of evildoers, neither be thou envious against the workers of iniquity. For they shall soon be cut down like the grass, and wither as the green herb. Trust in the Lord, and do good; so shalt thou dwell in the land, and verily thou shalt be fed'.

This seems so simple. When we trust in the Lord and keep His commandments, we are actually walking in humility. We should not be afraid of evil because we are obeying God and doing what He tells us to do. Humility is strength because we are submitted to God and allowing God's Word to cut down the workers of iniquity. We trust God because His word declares that if He spoke it, He will bring it to pass (Jeremiah 1:12, Ezekiel 12:25). In Isaiah 55:11 'so shall my word be that goeth forth out of my mouth; it shall not return unto me void, but it shall accomplish that which I please, and it shall prosper in the thing whereto I sent it.'

When you are humble, you MUST first agree with God. You must trust that He will hear and answer your prayers. The Lord will supply all of our needs. When God says you are blessed, agree with Him by saying, "I am blessed"! When God says you are healed, agree with Him by saying "I am healed"! Agree with God by saying "I am prosperous. I am wealthy. I am debt free and I owe no man anything. I am delivered. I am set free. I am a child of God"! This is true humility. I agree with God!

In Proverbs 3:27 'Withhold not good from them to whom it is due, when it is in the power of thine hand to do it'. We know right from wrong because of our spirit. Our spirit walks in love and humility. Our spirit is ready and equipped to be a blessing to many people. We have the power and the ability in our hands to do good. Let us all walk in humility, do them good and make them happy (Matthew 13:13-17)!

Chapter 6

Weakness or strength?....denial

It is hard on the flesh for a person to admit that they are wrong. Especially when they have confessed, professed and stood firm on what they thought was right or what they believed in. So many times, a person is simply walking in deception and has a 'closed mind' when it comes to apologizing. There are those who stand so strong in their beliefs that any sign of apologizing is a weakness. What is the root to this type of thinking? Pride. Pride will not let a person repent or ask for forgiveness. Pride will not even let a person admit a fault. In their mind, they have not done anything wrong. In Proverbs 21:2 'every way of a man is right in his own eyes, but the Lord pondereth the hearts'.

Some people will always give excuses to justify why they are right instead of admitting their faults. In Luke 16:15 'ye are they which justify yourselves before men; but God knoweth your hearts'. When a person is always trying to justify himself or explain his actions, most likely he is beginning to walk in pride. Pride wants to look right. The destruction occurs when a person feels they are always right in their actions, and then they will continue to do it. Ignorance will destroy you. They do not realize that they may be 'digging their own graves', thus they are becoming weaker and not stronger.

In James 1:14-15 'but every man is tempted, when is drawn away of his own lust, and enticed. Then when lust hath conceived, it bringeth forth sin: and sin, when it is finished, bringeth forth death'. If you think that apologizing is a weakness, you are actually initiating an inner, prideful emotion of being right. It is like being 'drawn away of your own lust' or your own desire. You desire to be right, therefore this desire, once conceived or believed upon will bring forth sin.

The sin starts when you have been drawn away by what you wanted to do. It's like Malachi 3:7 'even from the days of your fathers ye are gone away from mine ordinances, and have not kept them'. We are going away from God's order and from what God will have us to do. Now once sin is finished, it bringeth forth death. The spiritual death takes place first which is basically a separation from God. Something as simple as not willing to apologize can actually lead a person to a spiritual death. If you are not with God then you are against Him. As we all know that 'without God, we can do nothing' (John 15:5).

We need to understand the complete meaning of the word weak. Today's natural definition of weak is powerless, not physically strong or inadequate. This word has changed far away from its original meaning. In the Old Testament Hebrew bible, the word weak was defined as tenderhearted. The book of 2 Samuel 3:39 states 'and I am this day weak, though anointed king:' Weak meant to bear or carry. In Ezekiel 7:17 'all hands shall be feeble, and all knees shall be weak as water'. Weak also meant to be still, to mend and to be made whole. In Numbers 13:17-18 'And Moses sent them to spy out the land of Canaan, and said unto them, Get you up this way southward, and go up into the mountain:

And see the land, what it is; and the people that dwelleth therein, whether they be strong or weak, few or many'.

Weakness, in the Old Testament, was associated with meekness and being humble. As you can see, weakness can also be considered to be strength. Pride will make you feel as if any sign of submission is weak. It will make you think that admitting faults or an imperfection is weak. If you admit a mistake you are considered weak according to the world's system.

Let's look at the New Testament and Paul's attitude towards weakness. In the book of 2 Corinthians 12:9-10 Jesus said unto Paul, 'My grace is sufficient for thee: for my strength is made perfect in weakness'. Paul responded by saying: 'Most gladly therefore will I rather glory in my infirmities, that the power of Christ may rest upon me. Therefore I take pleasure in infirmities, in reproaches, in necessities, in persecutions, in distresses for Christ's sake, for when I am weak, then am I strong'. Paul recognized that when he was weak, tenderhearted, carrying burdens or when he was being mended then Jesus' strength was made perfect or complete. Therefore, when he was weak, in reality, he was strong. He was strong because the power of Christ, the anointed one and His anointing was resting upon him.

Do not deny your strength. Do not allow trying to be strong in the natural rob you of supernatural strength. This supernatural strength comes when you are weak or tenderhearted. Why? So that the purpose of the anointing, which is to remove burdens and destroy yokes, can manifest. Get your pride out the way. Remember that when you are weak you are actually strong.

In my own life, I always tried to appear strong. I always looked as if nothing bothered me. I did not want to cry at funerals or show any true emotions. I tried to hide those feelings. They made me feel like the world's definition of weak. In reality, I was living in denial. I was actually weak because I was too scared to face reality. In the bible, many people thought Paul lived in denial.

In 2 Corinthians 7:2 (when his name was Saul) Paul said 'receive us; we have wronged no man, we have corrupted no man, we have defrauded no man'. What did Paul say? He has not done 'anything' wrong? Wait a minute. Paul was the same persecutor of Christians, who in Acts 9:1-2 was even threatening the life of Jesus and the disciples. How can Paul have not done anything wrong? Well, this is how.

In Acts 9:3-6 he faced some real power. As he traveled the road to Damascus, a light came suddenly from heaven and flashed around him. This light was so powerful that it knocked Paul off his feet. Paul then heard a voice, looked up and asked who art thou, Lord? The voice responded, "I am Jesus whom thou persecutest". Paul's life was never the same. It was at that moment that he changed from Saul to Paul. Saul was the one who persecuted Christians. Saul was the lying, deceitful murderer who lived in denial. Once his name was changed to Paul, Saul died, and now Paul could freely say that he had wronged no man. Paul's mind and spirit had been renewed.

If you are reading this book, say this confession. I am in Christ; therefore I am a new creature. I am a new being that has never existed before. My past and all old things are behind me. All things are new in my life. The old person that I used to be has died. I have been redeemed. I am the redeemed of the Lord. I have wronged no man or woman. I am more than a conqueror. My hands have been washed clean by the blood of Jesus. I have a new attitude, a new way of living and a brand new way of thinking. I have a change of mind, a change of heart and a change of direction. I am blessed! My strength has been made perfect. In the name of Jesus I pray. Amen.

Chapter 7

A false balance....judgement

What is a false balance? It is like guessing your weight. Have you ever stood on a scale to see how much you weigh, but the marker indicator was slightly tilted to one side? This is when the marker is not in line with the "0". If you step on the scale at this time, your weight will not be accurate because the scale is off balance. This is the same effect that pride can have on a person's life. It gets you off balance.

Balance is the key to life. Balance keeps you from going too far to the left or too far to the right. It allows you to stay straight and focused. Where does pride come in? Pride is blinding. Pride allows you to see the situation only as it is right now. In Proverbs 11:1 'A false balance is an abomination to the Lord: but a just weight is his delight'.

Why is it an abomination? The amplified version of this scripture says 'a false balance and unrighteous dealings are extremely offensive and shamefully sinful to the Lord'. The Lord says that a false balance is equal to unrighteous dealings. Unrighteous dealings are things done without a covenant. These are things done without having a right to do them. It is when a person does something, but has no justified means or reasons as to why. It is like creating your own rules and regulations instead of obeying God's will.

The Lord is saying that you must look at the 'whole' picture and not just one side of the story. This is when judgement comes into existence. People make judgements everyday based on 'facts' only but not necessarily on the 'truth'. When the facts of a situation are carefully analyzed, you will get to the truth of the matter.

Pride is a straight and narrow path. Pride does not show you the whole story. It will not show you all of the future blessings to come. On a person's job, an employee may begin very slowly. He may appear that he is not catching on to an assignment or task. Since the boss is looking for immediate results, he may fire this employee. Three months later, this same employee has gone out and started his own business. Just because he started out slow with his old job does not mean he will end the same way. This employee could have been the type that wants to study his job first to make sure he understands his duties inside and out. He wants to put the company's vision in his mind. Now, to the natural mind it just looks like he is slow, however, he is simply preparing himself for greater things to come.

If you are always stuck on a 'first impression', you will never be able to see beyond today. Pride has already limited your thinking. You already have a false balance because you don't have the truth in you that will justify your thoughts or actions. You are operating by facts alone, which, by the way, can change.

Pride is strict. Pride is not forgiving or understanding. Pride has the attitude of 'it's my way or the highway'. These are reasons why pride is so destructive in this area of providing balance to a person's life. It tends to draw people away from the will of God. The word of God says that 'I can do all things through Christ which strengthened me' (Philippians 4:13). In the amplified version it says 'I have strength for all things in Christ who empowers me (I am ready for anything equal to anything through Him who infuses inner strength into me; I am self-sufficient in Christ's sufficiency)'.

So many people read this religiously, but I wonder did they really get a hold of what Paul was saying. Why did Paul say he could do all things? Paul recognized where the true source of his strength came from. Paul said that he was ready for anything equal to anything. He knew that Jesus Christ gave him strength to live everyday. He was completely satisfied because of Christ's sufficiency and because of what was in Him.

The anointing is what removes burdens and limits. There were no limits in Paul's life. There were no barriers that could not be broken through and by the anointing. Christ satisfied his actions, his thoughts and his beliefs. He had confidence in his ability because of Christ. Christ was his balance because it took the focus off him. If Paul walked in pride, then Paul would have been giving all the credit to himself and to what he could accomplish in his life instead of giving God the glory.

Balance is the key to life. What does that mean? Think about having a balanced diet. This requires a person to eat a certain percentage from each of the four basic food groups: dairy, vegetables, meat and bread. You also must intake a certain amount of calories, which vary, based on your height, weight, age and gender. If your diet is off balance, it can cause a chain reaction throughout your body. When we have balance in our lives, it allows us to take in the necessary nutrients to survive.

We need love, joy and peace. We need balance between work and home. The husband and wife need balance. We need discipline and understanding. In Ecclesiastes 3:1-9 it speaks of balance. 'To every thing there is a season, and a time to every purpose under the heaven. A time to break down, and a time to build up; A time to weep, and a time to laugh; a time to mourn, and a time to dance; A time to keep silence, and a time to speak'.

Without balance we risk not doing things under the direction of God. A false balance is similar to having your back turned to someone while not listening to reason. When we have balance we are more in tune with our inner man. We can listen and hear from God more effectively. How? Our hearts are yielded.

In Psalm 37:4 'delight thyself also in the Lord; and he shall give thee the desires of thine heart'. In the Hebrew bible, delight means to be soft or pliable. That means you are in a receiving state of mind. To be pliable is to be flexible or adaptable. You are flexible and adjustable. You are capable of being shaped or drawn out. When you have balance in your life, God can use you because your mind is flexible. We must renew our minds to a point to where we listen more. We will not be as quick to say no when the Holy Spirit is trying to minister to us. You will have understanding and discernment of spirit. We won't walk in judgement.

Pride will let your mind become one-sided because pride is concerned about what "I" want. Personally, I was what the world considers to be 'hard-headed'. I would make a decision, stick with it and would not even think about changing. I would have made up my mind to a point to where it was literally impossible for me to bend. I was so strict and disciplined. Being committed that way might not have been as bad if there was balance in my life. Balance would have softened my heart and helped me to realize that 'Ronnie Wells' may not know everything there is to know about life. I did not realize back then that 'Ronnie Wells' was actually ignorant. The bible says that fools don't listen and that fools reject wisdom (Proverbs 1:22-24).

Balance allows us to be submitted to God. It allows us look at 'both ends of the stick'. It will let us become fair in our daily communication with people when we know how it feels 'when the shoe is on the other foot'. I used to be quick to judge people, especially when they did something wrong. At the same time, people were very quick to judge me, so I guess I reaped what I sowed.

In Romans 3:22-23 'even the righteousness of God which is by faith of Jesus Christ unto all and upon all them that believe; for there is no difference: For all have sinned, and come short of the glory of God'. This is one scripture used by many people to justify their sins. They would say: "don't worry about sinning, because we all have done it". Where is the balance? It is very dangerous when we use a scripture from the bible out of context. This scripture meant that even though you have sinned you can still be righteous. The purpose of this scripture is to get your mind off the sin and to focus on the righteousness of God. This is balance.

Chapter 8

Resisting or enduring temptation...ignorance

In James 4:6-7 'but he giveth more grace. Wherefore he saith, God resisteth the proud, but giveth grace unto the humble. Submit yourselves therefore to God. Resist the devil, and he will flee from you'. Why does God resist the proud? The proud put more attention on other people, problems or situations than on God. Anything that is a resistance will go against the normal flow. In the Greek bible, resist also means to withstand or to fight against an object. Resistance sets up a challenge. Pride is a resistance. Therefore, the proud are standing against God.

On the other hand, the humble are meek, soft and pliable. The humble are open to God's grace and mercy. God gives grace to the humble because the humble are in a position to receive. God will resist the proud because the proud are fighting against Him. In Matthew 12:30 'He that is not with me is against me'.

Now, going back to James 4:7 God gives instructions. He says to submit yourselves to God. Why submit to God? You should submit to God so you can resist the devil and when you resist the devil, he will flee.

When you submit yourself to God, you are going under the mission of God. You are under the authority of God. This means that God has authority over your life. He becomes your leader, your guide and your protection.

With God having authority over your life, you will then be able to resist the devil. The devil knows the power and the authority that God has. The devil is no match to you when God is in control of your life. It is when you try to resist the devil alone that the challenges will come. 'He is proud, knowing nothing, but doting about questions and strifes of words, whereof cometh envy, strife, railings, evil surmisings, perverse disputings of men of corrupt minds, and destitute of the truth, supposing that gain is godliness: from such withdraw thyself' (1 Timothy 6:4-5).

The bible says the flesh is weak but the spirit is indeed willing. When we try to resist the devil alone, we are actually putting ourselves before God. Remember that we should submit to and be under the authority of God. Fighting your own battles, without permission from God, is being out of order. I feel in my spirit that a prideful person will be violating one of the 10 commandments: 'Thou shat have no other God before me'.

When we put problems before God, they are like 'gods' in our lives. Money problems are like 'gods'. Anything that has rule and authority over your life is like a god. What types of gods do you have in your life? Is alcohol your god? Is lust your god? Is material wealth your god? Is promotion and recognition your god? We must submit to our Heavenly Father, the one and only true God over our lives.

The topic of this chapter is resisting or enduring temptation. We know that resistance means to fight against, but what does endure mean? One definition of endure is to remain in existence in a state for a long time. It means to continue, to hold out or to persist. When I think about endure it reminds me of a marathon runner with great endurance to finish a race. Resistance to me is to protect yourself from opposition, while endurance is to press forward. Let's go to the scripture.

In 1 Corinthians 10:13 'There hath no temptation taken you but such as is common to man: but God is faithful, who will not suffer you to be tempted above that ye are able; but will with the temptation also make a way to escape, that ye may be able to bear it'.

In the Amplified bible 'For no temptation (no trial regarded as enticing to sin), (no matter how it comes or where it leads) has overtaken you and laid hold on you that is not common to man (that is, no temptation or trial has come to you that is beyond human resistance and that is not adjusted and adapted and belonging to human experience, and such as man can bear). But God is faithful (to his Word and to His compassionate nature), and He (can be trusted) not to let you be tempted and tried and assayed beyond your ability and strength of resistance and power to endure, but with the temptation He will (always) also provide the way out (the means of escape to a landing place), that you may be capable and strong and powerful to bear up under it patiently'. God says that you will always be above the temptation.

Temptation is simply a test or a trial of your emotions. Furthermore, it is a trial of your faith that tries to affect your emotions. God is saying, even though you will be tested, you will always be above it and you will always have a way to escape, so hang in there-you can bear it! I believe that as Christians, we give up too soon. We have to understand that according to this scripture, God said He is faithful to His word. We must come to realize that with God, we can do all things. This is why pride is such an enemy. When you walk in pride, God is in resistance to you, therefore, how can you resist the devil or his temptations without the faithfulness of God?

One way to escape temptation is we first must know that there is a way out. This is why we must submit to God first because He is our foundation. We cannot 'shake the devil' off unless we are rooted and grounded in His word. When we endure temptation, we continue forward by persisting and existing until the end. We already possess the strength necessary to pass the test. We simply need to use what we got.

Have you ever heard people say: "was that me, was that God or was that the devil" when they are trying to explain why hard times occur in their lives? In the book of James 1:13 'let no man say when he is tempted, I am tempted of God: for God cannot be tempted with evil, neither tempted he any man'. Did that answer your question? God does not tempt us with evil. Well, if God does not tempt us with evil does that mean that God can tempt us with good? We must first understand the original meaning of the word tempt. In the Old Testament in Genesis 22:1 'and it came to pass after these things, that God did tempt Abraham'. Now, in the book of James, God does not tempt any man but in Genesis, God tempted Abraham.

The Hebrew word for tempt is 'nacah' (naw-saw') which means to test; adventure, prove or try. The Amplified version of Genesis 22:1 'after these events, God tested and proved Abraham'.

As you can see, God did not tempt Abraham with evil, but God proved him. God allows us to prove our worth to Him. In other words, God wants to see 'what we are made of'. When a person is buying a new car they normally take it for a test drive in order to give the automobile an opportunity or a chance to prove to us if it is worth buying or not. So likewise, temptations in our lives are to strengthen us. It gives us a chance to test our ability, to test our faith and to test the word of God that we stand on everyday.

Remember the story of Job. I hear people say all the time that God turned Job over to the devil to teach him a lesson. In Job 1:1-4 he was considered a man who completely reverenced God and hated evil. He was a very prosperous man who loved his family dearly. He loved his family so much, to a point, that in order to make sure they were protected, he brought offerings to God everyday (verse 5). Every time he came before God, he would bring an offering and make a covenant with God to protect his children. Now, we look at this as an act of faith, but in reality, it was an act of fear. Job was afraid of losing his children so he went before God everyday with the same prayer, the same offering and the same covenant. Job gave offerings and made a covenant with God everyday, just in case the first one did not work.

As Christians, we should only need to make a covenant with God one time and stand on that covenant. We should stand on that covenant until the word of God, that we are confessing, comes into existence. When we are asking God the same thing everyday, it may be an indication that we do not truly believe in our first prayer. Our first prayer should be, "Lord bless me". Our next prayer should then be, "Lord, thank you for blessing me. Lord, I believe I have received. Lord, thank you for the manifestation".

Now, continuing with the story of Job, there was a day when the sons of God came to present themselves before the Lord, Satan came also (verses 6-12) to ask permission to tempt Job. The Lord began to brag about Job, letting Satan know that Job was a perfect and upright man. He even asked Satan have you considered my servant Job. In today's language, God said: 'take your best shot'. Contrary to traditional thinking, God did not turn Job over to the devil. God only tempted or allowed Job to prove himself. Satan knew God protected Job. Satan also knew Job's rights, however, Job did not know. In verse 12 the Lord said 'Behold, all that he (Job) hath is in thy power'. This meant that Job's power was given to the devil. How? Job turned himself over to the devil through his continual offerings, which only put fear in him.

The bible tells us not to give place to the devil. We give the devil a place in our life mainly through our confessions. When we continue to speak doubt, fear and unbelief, we are actually giving strength to the devil. We are actually in agreement with Him; therefore we have given the devil a place or a right to be in our lives. This is one small form of pride. It was pride because Job was resisting God.

While Job was being tormented by the devil, Job failed to put God back in remembrance of the covenant offerings he had made. In Job 1:21-22 Job said 'the Lord gave, and the Lord hath taken away; blessed be the name of the Lord. In all this Job sinned not, nor charged or accused God foolishly'. Also, in Job 3:25 he also said 'for the thing which I greatly feared is come upon me, and that which I was afraid of is come unto me'. Job admitted that it was his own fault that Satan over-came him. It was his fault that he did not resist the devil's temptation by proving his worth to God. Job fell to the temptation and failed the test.

People today seem to fail the test of temptation. They look at temp-tation as a situation that is against them. It appears overpowering. If a person is not prepared for a test, then of course they will have some sort of fear. Especially when they do not know if they will pass or fail. However, when a person is prepared, they should have no fear about temptations. Temptation is only another opportunity for them to prove themselves.

Temptation is only a test. It all depends on the individual. I once heard that if you slap two men, one man has the opportunity to be defeated and the other has the opportunity to become the heavyweight boxing champ of the world. What is the difference? One may fall to temptation and one will prove himself and pass the test.

Let's examine a couple of bible stories of how to pass the test of temptation. In the book of Daniel 6:1-28 is the story of how Daniel escaped the lion's den unharmed. King Darius appointed Daniel one of three presidents over the kingdom of the Chaldeans. The other two presidents were extremely jealous of him because Daniel was considered distinguished over them all. Of course, they could not find any reason or faults of Daniel that they could use as a reason to see him removed as president.

They then convinced King Darius to establish a royal statue or law making it illegal to pray. If someone were caught praying, the penalty would be death by being thrown into a den of lions. They knew that Daniel prayed faithfully 3 times a day or more. Once King Darius signed the law, they just knew they had Daniel right where they wanted him. Did this new law stop Daniel from praying? No, it didn't. Daniel continued to pray and give thanks to God, regardless of the law that was passed. In 2 Corinthians 3:6 'for the letter killeth, but the spirit giveth life'.

So many Christians compromise their relationship with God for a relationship with the world. So many Christians are in bondage to people to a point that they are even too afraid or too embarrassed to pray or acknowledge God in public places. Daniel was not going to allow anything to separate him from the love of God.

Once King Darius was informed that Daniel violated his law to not pray, he was ordered to be cast into a den of lions. Now, so many people read this story religiously. People think that once Daniel was thrown into the lion's den that he began to pray to God and then God delivered him. People think that Daniel developed faith while he was in the den.

No. Daniel had faith in God before facing the lion. In Daniel 6:13 (Amplified bible) 'Then they said before the king, That Daniel, who is one of the exiles from Judah, does not regard or pay any attention to you, O king, or to the decree that you have signed, but makes his petition three times a day'. Daniel was not even thinking about a so-called law. Daniel prayed continually to God. The king, in Daniel 6:16 even said to Daniel 'May your God, Whom you are serving continually, deliver you'! Daniel was building his faith and establishing a solid foundation with God.

Let's watch how God delivered him. In Daniel 6:19-22 'Then the king arose very early in the morning, and went in haste unto the den of lions. And when he came to the den, he cried with a lamentable voice unto Daniel: and the king spake and said to Daniel, O Daniel, servant of the living God, is thy God, whom thou servest continually, able to deliver thee from the lions? Then said Daniel unto the king, O king, live forever. My God hath sent his angel, and hath shut the lions' mouth, that they have not hurt me: forasmuch as before him innoceny was found in me; and also before thee, O king, have I done no hurt'. No weapon formed against Daniel was able to prosper. Why? Daniel had faith in God before the lion's den.

God supplied Daniel with everything that he needed before the temptation. God will never allow you to go through any test, trial or temptation without giving you the necessary equipment to survive.

In Daniel 3:1-30 is the story of Shadrach, Meshach, Abednego and the fiery furnace. King Nebuchadnezzar made golden images that he and his people worshipped as gods. Any person that did not bow down and worship this image would be put to death immediately by being thrown into a burning furnace of fire. Once King Nebuchadnezzar found out that there were men, who did not compromise their belief in God, to worship his god, he had them arrested and brought before his court.

In Daniel 3:16-17 'Shadrach, Meshach, and Abednego, answered and said to the king, O Nebuchadnezzar, we are not careful to answer thee in this matter. If it be so, our God whom we serve is able to deliver us from the burning fiery furnace, and he will deliver us out of thine hand, O king'. These men had faith in God. They did not know when, how or where but they knew that God can and that God will deliver them. They had faith in God before the fire.

In Daniel 3:24-25 'Then Nebuchadnezzar the king was astonied, and rose up in haste, and spake, and said unto his counselors, Did not we cast three men bound into the midst of the fire? They answered and said unto the king, True, O king. He answered and said, Lo, I see four men loose, walking in the midst of the fire, and they have no hurt; and the form of the fourth is like the Son of God'. Hallelujah!

Not only was God able to give them the faith they needed to escape the temptation of the fiery furnace, but also He was willing to get in the fire with them. God is good. In Jeremiah 1:12 God said that 'He is alert and active to watch over His word to perform it'. If God spoke it, He will do it. His word will not return void. God promised Shadrach, Meshach, and Abednego that He would never leave them nor forsake them. God was at their side before the fire, during the fire, and when they went "through" the fire. They went "through" the fire! They went "through" the fire! They did not set up a camp in the midst of their trial. They kept the faith in God to deliver them and God did just what he said he would do.

Now, ask yourself a question: Are you resisting or enduring temptation? Are you putting up with a destructive situation or do you have faith in God to deliver you? God promised in His word that he would not allow you to suffer or be tempted above what you are able to bear and will always have a way for you to escape. Always. Don't ignore the path God has set for you. Don't put up with the devil. Don't ignore the word of God.

How do we respond when are faced with temptations? What type of attitude should we have? What do we do? In Romans 8:28 'and we know that all things work together for good to them that love God, to them who are the called according to his purpose'. This is another religious, traditional way of thinking. People use this scripture to formulate situations and circumstances to justify their means. In other words, they try to make up or devise reasons why things, good or bad, happen in their lives in order to place the blame on God.

Now, in Romans 8:26 'likewise the Spirit also helpeth our infirmities: for we know not what we should pray for as we ought: but the Spirit himself maketh intercession for us with groanings which cannot be uttered'. This means that we are praying in tongues in our weaknesses. In verse 27 'and he that searcheth the hearts knoweth what is the mind of the Spirit, because he maketh intercession for the saints according to the will of God'. Here, the Holy Spirit knows what our intent was and what was in our hearts from the beginning "before" we began to pray. In verse 28 'and we know that all things work together for good…' These scriptures are literally saying that praying in tongues, intercession, belief or faith in God along with the Holy Spirit is the reason why things work together for our good. All the things of God work together for our good.

A car wreck, hard times, unemployment, sickness, disease, financial problems or any like situations or circumstances do not work together for our good. The only things that work for your good are the things of God, which were intentionally designed and purposed in a believer's heart. Pride looks for excuse to justify their means. Pride wants to blame God or any other person but themselves. Pride does not want to face or resist temptation. Pride will not admit that seedtime and harvest was in place. Pride does not recognize that you reap what you sow. Pride hides from temptation. Pride cannot pass the test.

Chapter 9

Rebellion. Fools don't listen...stubborn

One type of person that I do not like to associate with is a "know it all". Every subject that comes up in conversation, they always seem to have a comment. They have seen every play, heard every song, been to every state and know about every country. They have watched every television show. They can predict the weather and even know all about history. It just amazes me. The humorous part is whether they are right or wrong, they always seem to have a comment.

As you can probably imagine, how can you teach someone that already thinks they know everything? You can't. Since pride is all about "I" it is almost impossible for that person to receive advice, wisdom, criticism or anything that may seem to contradict or go against their knowledge. In James 4:6 'God resisteth the proud but giveth grace to the humble'. To resist means to withstand or to fight against an object. There is a resistance or an opposing force in a person with pride. There is a barrier in the way when there is resistance.

Pride is that barrier. Pride stops up or hinders the flow of God. God resists the proud but is able to give grace to the humble. How? The humble are in a position to receive the wisdom of God. There is not a struggle for God to show his grace and mercy to the humble. In the book of Proverbs 1:7 Solomon said 'the fear of the Lord is the beginning of knowledge: but fools despise wisdom and instruction'. A person that has resistance to advice is known as a fool. Fools do not listen to advice.

In the first part of this verse Solomon said the fear of the Lord is the beginning of knowledge. Once knowledge begins, a person should have the reverential fear or respect for the Lord. Now, this is getting deep. If you do not receive advice or criticism well, if knowledge is not in the beginning, God said you are disrespecting Him. You are not operating in the fear of the Lord.

In Proverbs 9:10 'the fear of the Lord is the beginning of wisdom: and the knowledge of the holy is understanding'. We must understand what it truly means to fear the Lord. When we fear the Lord, we must respect Him. We must acknowledge His presence in our lives as the creator of all things. Man was formed from the dust of the ground and did not begin to live until God breathed the breath of life in Him. God is the one that gives us life. He gives us health and strength to make it from day to day. God is a big God! The grace and mercy of God is a gift to us. God does so much for us. We should at least thank Him for his loving kindness.

We must recognize and respect who He is in our lives. We must give God the reverential fear and respect that He deserves. When we begin to fear the Lord, wisdom can begin. Wisdom is the ability to use knowledge. Wisdom is a higher level of knowledge. Wisdom comes from inside our spirit and flows out into the world.

Wisdom has a solid foundation. This foundation is based on the word of God. In the book of 1 Corinthians 2:7 'But we speak the wisdom of God in a mystery, even the hidden wisdom, which God ordained before the world unto our glory'. If we do not fear the Lord, we will never be able to know what God had ordained for us before we were born. We will never know our true purpose in life. If we do not acknowledge God then how can the wisdom of God be given to us? We miss out on so much when we do not fear the Lord. It should not be a struggle to fear the Lord.

There are things that we should or should not do just from proper home training. Do not forget about who God is in your life. 'My soul shall make her boast in the Lord: the humble shall hear thereof, and be glad' (Psalms 34:2).

God is the Alpha and the Omega, the beginning and the end. Since God is the beginning, and knowledge is in the beginning, then to despise or reject knowledge is to despise or reject God. God is the great I am. God knows all things. If people think they know everything then that person is trying to place themselves as gods. The very first commandment clearly states 'Thou shalt have no other god before me'. Once you exalt yourself higher than you should, then you are actually establishing yourself as a god. Walking in pride, in the eyes of God, is the same as having another god before Him. What in your life is taking the place of God? What advice do you not want or need?

Remember that we can do nothing without God. Man was only dust until God breathed the breath of life in him. We still need that breath today. Just because you have oxygen today, does not mean you won't need it tomorrow. So why do people think that just because we have knowledge today, then we won't need it tomorrow? Resistance to advice grieves the Holy Spirit. Everything we need and everything God has for us has been given to us through his spirit. In Proverbs 20:27 'the spirit of man is the candle of the Lord'. God uses our spirit to lead us and to guide us.

If we reject the Holy Spirit we are actually rejecting God's plan and method to teach us. Remember that 'God is a spirit, and he that worship the Father must worship him in spirit and in truth' (John 4:23). We must worship him in spirit, which has to be open to God in truth or in reality. We receive wisdom, healing, deliverance, prosperity and even our salvation through our spirit. It is almost like saying you do not need oxygen in our heart or blood in our veins if we reject the Holy Spirit. If we reject knowledge and wisdom, we reject the Holy Spirit. We then reject God. We must drop pride and walk in humility. God gives grace to the humble.

I used to be that person that knew it all. I thought I had the answer to every problem. I was an honor graduate in high school and I was almost always the smartest student in class. It was hard to tell me I was wrong. This stubborn attitude settled in my spirit. I became rebellious and defensive if someone tried to prove me wrong. Why? Pride.

I always thought that a person who could not answer a question was stupid. We called them dumb. Let me add balance to that statement. I was walking in pride; thus, I felt that people without common sense were ignorant. I have learned now that ignorance is not stupidity, but ignorance is not knowing. There are things that we don't know because we may not have experienced it yet. The best way to know something is to ask. In an earlier chapter, I talked about pride not letting a person ask for anything. Pride wanted to solve its own problem instead of allowing God to work through someone else to bless me.

Personally, I did not ask questions because of pride. I did not want to appear stupid, ignorant or dumb. One day I heard someone say that the only dumb or stupid question is the one that you don't ask. This is really true ignorance because we 'ignore' or reject knowledge. In Hosea 4:6 'my people are destroyed for lack of knowledge: because thou hast rejected knowledge, I will also reject thee'.

When we reject knowledge, we create a resistance to what could be our breakthrough in life. If someone were on a hot and dry desert land, would he reject water? If someone were in a famine-stricken country, would he reject food? I doubt it because they recognize that these things are what they need to live. So likewise, we must come to the point of realizing that knowledge and wisdom are vital to our lives. Why reject something that helps us live?

Recently, my faith was tested in this area of rejecting knowledge. I was having bible study, and I asked someone to explain a scripture to me in their own words. In 2 Peter 3:8 'but beloved, be not ignorant of this one thing, that one day is with the Lord as a thousand years, and a thousand years as one day'. Well, they explained the scripture in detail, and used good examples, however, I still did not understand. Normally, my pride would have told them to stop trying to explain because I was not receiving what they were saying. I would have stopped listening and tuned them out. It would have been easier on my mind to end the conversation rather than try and comprehend that scripture. This time, I dropped my pride, placed myself in a receiving position and received the knowledge they were imparting into my life.

Pride had robbed me of receiving so much knowledge and wisdom that God had for me. When I looked at the scripture we were discussing, I noticed that it said to 'be not ignorant' of this one thing. The scripture even warned me not to be ignorant, but to recognize that one-year with God is equivalent to one thousand years on the earth. I also looked at Psalm 90:4 'for a thousand years in thy sight are but as yesterday when it is past, and as a watch in the night'. When I opened my spirit to receive 2 Peter, now the Lord was able to show me even more revelation.

Don't be too hasty or too quick to reject knowledge. Many Christians are so quick to use the term 'I don't receive that' when they begin to hear something that does not agree with how they think or feel. I do believe in guarding your heart from evil communication, however, don't let pride get in the way to a point that you 'don't receive' any advice that does not agree with yours. Make sure you have a clear understanding of what is being said before you become so quick to reject it.

'Study to show thyself approved unto God, a workman that needeth not to be ashamed, rightly dividing the word of truth' (2 Timothy 2:15). In Psalm 90:12 'so teach us to number our days, that we may apply our hearts unto wisdom'. In other words, do not take one day for granted, because we need to always be in a position of expectation.

Why did I not want to listen? One reason was that I spoke too fast. The bible says in James 1:19 'wherefore, my beloved brethren, let every man be swift to hear, slow to speak, slow to wrath'. God gave us two ears and one mouth, so apparently this may mean we should listen twice as much. When a person's mouth is constantly 'running', they tend to lose opportunity to receive much wisdom and knowledge. They are never in a receiving position. We should learn to be directed by God when we speak instead of being driven by our emotions.

Another reason why I did not want to listen was the fact that I lacked patience. One definition of patience is to wait, to remain the same or to endure without complaint. The bible says to acknowledge God or to ask God first and He will direct our paths. I did not have time to wait on God for an answer. I felt I already knew the answer anyway so God would probably just tell me what I already know. This was pride. I really had no real way of knowing that those words I spoke would be acceptable to God. I was walking in the flesh, so I did not have the mind of Christ.

In Ecclesiastes 3:1 'to every thing there is a season, and a time to every purpose under the heaven'. 'A time to keep silence, and a time to speak' (verse 7). I did not wait on the right time to speak, but instead, I reacted based on my emotions and based on how I felt. I was very stubborn and did not listen to reason. It was my way or the highway.

The problem was not in the sender of the message, but the problem was with my inability to receive. The message may have been a soft, wind of advice, but pride turned that soft wind into a storm. People tend to take things the wrong way or insinuate something that was not said. How does this happen? How or what makes us 'blow things out of proportion'? In Job 8:2 'How long wilt thou speak these things? And how long shall the words of thy mouth be like a strong wind'? The words of your mouth are just like a strong wind. The more you talk, the stronger the wind will get. This is probably how the phrase 'stirring up things' was started. In Exodus 23:1 'Thou shalt not raise a false report'. Do not bring up a conversation that is not true. Do not stir up a situation that has been settled.

Now, based on what a person is saying will determine the type of wind that will blow. In Ephesians 4:14 'That we henceforth be no more children, tossed to and fro, and carried about with every wind of doctrine, by the sleight of men, and cunning craftiness, whereby they lie in wait to deceive'. Children have a tendency to believe everything that they hear. Their minds are young and in the stage of formation.

When people still act like children, they too are subject to be tossed around. If there is no solid foundation about what and why you believe in a certain subject, then the 'winds of doctrine' will carry you. This is why a person must have a full understanding of what was said before they are driven to respond. When we react to something being said to us, the bible says that we need to grow up. We are still acting like children because we have no foundation. We have no support or trust in our own belief.

The words of our mouth are like a strong wind. The words that we speak have power. Our words can move mountains or calm a raging sea. On the other hand, our words have the ability to create mountains and storms in our lives. In the book of Mark 4:37-41 'And there arose a great storm of wind, and the waves beat into the ship, so that it was now full. And he (Jesus) was in the hinder part of the ship, asleep on a pillow: and they awake him, and say unto him, Master, carest thou not that we perish? And he arose, and rebuked the wind, and said unto the sea. Peace, be still. And the wind ceased, and there was a great calm. And he said unto them, Why are ye so fearful? How is it that ye have no faith? And they feared exceedingly, and said one to another. What manner of man is this, that even the wind and the sea obey him!'

This is the story of when Jesus rebuked the wind and the sea. Now, this sounds like Jesus was talking to the sea or did he? Yes he did. The word says that he told the sea: 'Peace, be still'. During one of our 5a.m. morning prayer sessions, with my Barrier Breaker prayer partners, the Lord revealed to Kelvin the meaning of this scripture. Danny and I were just rejoicing over this revelation.

In order to get a full understanding of this revelation, we must look at this story as told in the gospel according to St. Matthew. In the book of Matthew 8:23-27 'And when he (Jesus) was entered into a ship, his disciples followed him. And, behold, there arose a great tempest in the sea, insomuch that the ship was covered with the waves: but he was asleep.

And his disciples came to him, and awoke him, saying, Lord, save us: we perish. And he saith unto them, Why are ye fearful, O ye of little faith? Then he arose, and rebuked the winds and the sea; and there was a great calm. But the men marvelled, saying, What manner of man is this, that even the winds and the sea obey him!'

Notice what Jesus did when the disciples came to him. Jesus asked them a question: 'Why are ye fearful, O ye of little faith?' Firstly, Jesus calmed the disciples. He spoke peace to the disciples. In Mark 4:39 Jesus said, 'Peace, be still'. In actuality, Jesus told the disciples, 'peace'. The Hebrew definition for peace is shalom. It means to be safe in mind and body. Peace means to be complete or to make amends. Peace means to restore. There is nothing missing, nothing broken or nothing lacking from your life. The Greek definition for peace is eirene. This means prosperity, oneness, quietness or rest.

Based on these definitions, peace is a covenant word. The Lord revealed through Kelvin that Jesus was not talking to the sea when he said peace. He was speaking to the disciples. He wanted the disciples to have peace in their spirit. The disciples lacked faith in God. Jesus was putting them back in remembrance of the word of God. They needed peace. Jesus told them that they were safe in their mind and body.

He told them that they were complete and he told them they would be restored. There would not be anything missing, broken or lacking from their lives. Jesus let them know they would be prosperous and whole. He wanted them to be quiet and to rest. Jesus could now take care of the storm. Little did the disciples know, the storm was in their mind. The longer they had fear in their hearts, the stronger the winds blew.

Remember, in Job 8:2 'the words of thy mouth will be like a strong wind'. The disciples spoke words of fear that produced strong winds. The more they feared, the stronger the winds became, to a point that they produced a storm. This great storm of wind and waves is what beat the ship. It was not until Jesus spoke peace to the disciples that the winds began to cease. At this point, Jesus then told the sea 'be still'.

So many times, we stir up 'winds of doctrines' in our minds through negative thinking. The problem gets worse when we begin to speak these thoughts. We must not allow the devil to deceive us into evil thinking. We must begin to guard our hearts. We must be careful of the things we say, watch or listen to. The mouth, the eyes and the ears are avenues that the devil tries to use to tempt us. If he is able to put fear in us, then it will set in our heart. We must continue to submit ourselves to God, first, and then resist the devil. We must speak peace, first. We must set our atmosphere by speaking the word of God over every situation and over every circumstance in our lives. Let the peace of God rule in our hearts and not the turmoil and winds of doctrine from the devil. Seek God first.

I thank God that I am free from pride. I am now pliable and open to receive the knowledge and wisdom that God has for me. Ecclesiastes 12:13 'let us hear the conclusion of the whole matter: Fear God, and keep his commandments: for this is the whole duty of man'. In the Amplified version 'All has been heard; the end of the matter is: Fear God (revere and worship Him, knowing that He is) and keep his commandments, for this is the whole of man (the full, original purpose of his creation, the object of God's providence, the root of character, the foundation of all happiness, the adjustment to all inharmonious circumstances and conditions under the sun) and the whole (duty) for every man'.

In summary, listen to every word that is being said until the end, respect God, and do what he tells you to do since this is your assignment. After it is all said and done, we still must respect God. It does not matter what the situation was, who started it or how it ended, the bottom line is still to respect God. Let the fear of the Lord dwell in us. Let the fear of the Lord become our peacemaker. There are many things, which we would not do, if we feared the Lord. So many times, we think that just because we are out of the sight of people that we are out of the sight of God. If you are alone, you should still respect God. Even if you are on a desert island and surrounded by all types of sin, we should still respect God. Let the conclusion of everything be to respect God.

Chapter 10

Forgive and forget...anger

Think before you speak. My mama used to tell me to count from one to ten before I responded to people if I was mad at them. (Sometimes counting did not help, but, I did make all A's in mathematics throughout school.) In James 1:19 says 'wherefore, my beloved brethren, let every man be swift to hear, slow to speak, slow to wrath:' I once heard this phrase: Life is 10% of what happens to you and 90% is how you react. If we took the time to look at both sides of the story, we will find that the things we are upset about are not worth it at all.

We are made in the image of God and God is a spirit. The fruit of the spirit is love, joy, peace, longsuffering, gentleness, goodness, faith, meekness, temperance: against such there is no law. It is in us to love. Hate or anger is not a fruit of the spirit. Unforgiveness should not be a part of your life. We must forgive and forget. They both go together. Many people say I will forgive you, but I'll never forget. Well, in reality they truly have not forgiven. In Philippians 3:13 Paul said 'to forget those things which are behind, and reach forth unto those things which are before'. If you do not forget the past you cannot reach to the future.

In James 5:16 'confess your faults one to another, and pray for one another, that ye may be healed. The effectual fervent prayer of a right-eous man availeth much'. An effectual, heartfelt prayer brings forth power. There is no healing power in anger. Anger is the power of the devil that will send you straight to hell. We will reap what we sow. When we pray for another person, someone else will pray for us. In the book of Luke 6:37 'Judge not, and ye shall not be judged: condemn not, and ye shall not be condemned: forgive and ye shall be forgiven'. Let's release blessings out of our mouth and out of our hearts-not cursings (James 3:10). Love thy brother; forgive and forget. We must 'bear ye one another's burdens, and so fulfill the law of Christ' (Galatians 6:2).

Pride will keep a person from admitting their faults or wrong doings. In turn they will not repent, they won't ask for forgiveness nor will they forgive others. If people were not able to admit their faults, then why would they repent? A prideful person already feels he has no need to repent. He has not done anything wrong. Remember the story of Paul we talked about in an earlier chapter. Paul said in 2 Corinthians 7:2 'receive us; we have wronged no man'. This sound like pride to me since Paul had many Christians killed and murdered. However, remember this, Paul's name was formerly Saul. Saul was the person who committed those wrong acts, but on the road to Damascus (Acts 13:1-9), Saul was filled with the Holy Ghost and his name was changed to Paul. Paul took on a new identity. So yes, Paul had wronged no man. Paul had been transformed by renewing his mind by the Holy Spirit.

I realize that it is hard on the flesh to forgive someone who has done something wrong to you. It is also hard on the flesh to ask for forgive-ness when you have done something wrong to someone else. We must forgive because it is a commandment from God. In Mark 11:25-26 'if ye have ought against any, ye must forgive so that the father will forgive you'. In Matthew 5:22-24 'if you are angry with your brother, without cause you should bring a gift to the altar in remembrance of him'. If we still obeyed that commandment, many altars would probably be loaded with tithes and offerings.

Just think about the number of times you have been upset or have held a grudge against someone. A person that walks in pride might have a hard time forgiving even one time. In the book of Matthew 18, Jesus was talking to his disciples about overcoming offenses, being supportive of friends, the church and walking in agreement with others. Peter came to him in Matthew 18:21 and made a very sarcastic statement, 'How often shall my brother sin against me, and I forgive him? till seven times?' He basically said, is seven times enough? Will that satisfy you since you are all into this forgiveness mode? Jesus responded and said— No, seven times is not quite enough. Let's make it seventy times seven.

One reason why Jesus gave that number was because it represented an unlimited number of times you should forgive. Never put a boundary on what you will be willing to do or not do. Just imagine the stress on a person's brain they would have if they held all that anger inside of them. The veins will start showing out their forehead.

Holding grudges inside your heart can be like cancer, which will literally destroy a person from the inside out. In Ephesians 4:26 'be ye angry and sin not: let not the sun go down upon your wrath'. Never go to bed mad. The Lord did realize there would be situations and circumstances to arise in your life that would make you angry. We should not respond in a sinful manner. Only your flesh is angry, however, the spirit should be ready, willing and able to forgive.

In Romans 12:2 'and be not conformed to this world: but be ye transformed by the renewing of your mind, that ye may prove what is that good, and acceptable, and perfect, will of God'. Do not be conformed to this prideful sin called anger. Do not let anger conform you. Don't even go to bed with it on your mind. Before you go to sleep, you will have to forgive.

Here are some helpful tips. In Proverbs 14:29 'he that is slow to wrath is of great understanding: but he that is hasty of spirit exalteth folly'. Before you react, be sure you have understanding first. Remember that we cannot control another person's actions but we can always control our reactions. Also, in Proverbs 15:1 'a soft answer turneth away wrath: but grievous words stir up anger'.

Don't go 'blow for blow' but become a person of integrity and honor and try to bring peace into your situation. Most times, when you lower your voice and humble your attitude, the other person will truly sound loud and ignorant. Proverbs 15:18 'a wrathful man stirreth up strife: but he that is slow to anger appeaseth strife'. The Amplified version reads 'a hot-tempered man stirs up strife, but he who is slow to anger appeases contention'.

There is a phrase that says 'misery loves company'. 'Only by pride cometh contention: but with the well advised is wisdom' (Proverbs 13:10). People who are mad, upset or depressed are only seeking someone to share in their pity party. They love to argue because it will bring the other individual into their world of discomfort. Do not fall for it. Drop your pride, forgive and forget.

Chapter 11

Love thy neighbor...excuses

Faithfulness is a word that has more power than we even realize. Faithfulness means that regardless of a situation or circumstance, we will continue to be faithful. We will still complete whatever task is at hand. A faithful man will complete his task at all costs. He will not come up with excuses or reasons why he could not fulfill a goal. We need to get away from always using excuses. It does not matter whether it is a good excuse or a bad excuse. We should begin to learn what it means to be faithful. A faithful man will recognize the problem, change and make the necessary adjustments to continue their mission.

An example of a faithful man is how he would react if he had a flat tire on his way to work. Instead of calling his employer and saying he won't be on time, their mentality changes. His mentality will be 'if I have to run, leave the car and the flat tire, and come back and get it later, I still have to be at work on time'. He does not have time to give excuses for not doing something.

Now, what does this have to do with pride? A prideful spirit will come up with excuses and reasons to justify why they did or did not do certain things. They will always have an alibi to use so it won't look as if they failed. They tend to say 'here's the reason why I did or did not do it'.

One area of my life that was almost destroyed, due to pride, was my relationship with my mother and father. I lived with my father, and I must admit, he was a good man and a good daddy to me. While he was alive, he always worked 2 or 3 jobs. He always provided all of my needs. Even though we lived in the projects, we were very happy or in other words, content.

However, on the weekends (and several weekdays) my father drank a lot of beer and liquor. He even gave me some alcohol when I was a child (to put me to sleep, of course). Apparently, he didn't see much harm in giving a little 'squig' to his little baby boy. Little did he know that the seed of alcoholism he planted in me at age 2 grew into a mighty mountain. At the age of 13, I began developing the skills, characteristics and nature of an alcoholic. I would even drink before and after school. I would drink even every weekend.

I began going to clubs with some of my older associates. I became labeled as a "functional alcoholic" because even though I was a heavy drinker, I was still able to function. I was an honor graduate at Griffin High School and an honor graduate at Branell College. Even at my place of employment, I was able to achieve a respectable status and position. I was never fired from any job. I have always maintained a very stable employment history. My work performance was extremely exceptional because my goal was to exceed in everything that I did.

My co-workers only knew me at work. However, when I came home, I drank beer and liquor until I literally passed out. The next morning, I was always at work very early, and was almost always on time. I was determined to be faithful to my job. When I was approached, (by people who knew me), about my drinking, I would use my father as an excuse. I would say, "My father was an alcoholic". "Alcoholism was hereditary in my family". "I have been drinking since age 2 and it was too hard to stop".

As hard as it may seem, I was walking in pride. I refused to admit I had a problem or that I could have been the problem. I was the one who made the decision to continue drinking. At any time, I could have looked in the mirror and decided to change my life. Instead, I waited until I was 27 years old before I finally chose to change my life. During those years, I mistreated and disrespected people. I did so many evil, wicked things. My 'excuse' every time was that I was an alcoholic. My excuse was pride.

The reason I am telling this story is the effect of pride in my life, mixed with alcohol, destroyed my relationship with my mother for many years. Since I lived with my father, I did not spend much time with my mother. I would visit her in the summer and also during various holidays. My mother lived in Dublin, GA, which was about 120 miles away from my home in Griffin. Even though from time to time we did see each other, the relationship with her was not the same as the relationship with my daddy.

Firstly, I discovered at a late age that my daddy lied to me. He told me that my mother left him for another man. He told me that she was an alcoholic and always wasted their money every weekend. He even told me that she would even sell food out of the refrigerator in order to have money for beer and liquor. All of these accusations about my mother caused me to form this negative image about her. I did not know any better. I was only about 2 years old when she left. My whole entire life, I carried this grudge inside against my mother because of what my father said. Apparently, he did not realize the negative influence he had on my life by telling me all those things about my mother. My mother and I never had a consistent relationship because of these reasons. I just did not trust her based on what my dad said.

Secondly, this grudge that I had against my mother was never dealt with. My mother or I never took the initiative to sit down and talk about her past. I never had any understanding as to why my mother acted the way that my father said she did. There was no balance given in that situation. All she knew to do was to buy my love. She found out the hard way that money could not buy true love and happiness. I grew up accepting the gifts, however, my heart was far from them. I never appreciated anything that she did for me. I realize now that my mother was trying to satisfy my flesh instead of satisfying my spirit. I needed her to tell me that she was sorry for leaving my daddy. I needed her to explain what happened between her and my dad. My spirit and soul were empty and starving for her affection. I needed those answers and I needed them immediately.

Since I did not have a steady relationship with my mother, I never had a steady relationship with women. I used and abused them. I lied, cheated, fornicated, and did so many ungodly things. My excuse every time was that I was an alcoholic or that I did not love my mother so I did not know how to love other women.

What happened to faithfulness over the years? Pride blocked my faithfulness. I mistreated those women because that was my decision. Pride began to grow while I was giving these excuses for drinking and for my personal relationships. Pride had blinded me. Pride had me looking at other people and other factors as the problem. Oh no, I could not consider blaming myself. It would not look good if I blamed myself.

I have learned how to 'honor my mother and my father' (Exodus 20:12). I honored them, not only by giving them respect, but I gave them authority and dominion to make decisions over my life. I begin to show trust, love and commitment. As soon as I dropped pride, and begin to change my attitude towards my mother, family and friends, I was then able to open my heart to other people. I begin to show signs of true friendship. I stopped holding grudges, being angry and mistreating people.

My mother and I finally decided to sit down and discuss my anger and talk about exactly what was driving it. She had no idea that I was upset at her for leaving. She explained that both her and my father were alcoholics. My father was very abusive at times to a point that she feared for her life. She actually thought she would die. Alcoholism almost took her life as the result of a motorcycle accident. When she decided to leave my father, it was actually an act of her love for me. She knew that although my father had a problem with alcoholism, he was extremely faithful to his children. She was confident that my dad would take care of me, and overall, she was right.

My mother was only 15 years old when she married my father, who was 43. Her entire childhood was taken away when she became a teenage mother. Therefore, she felt that she had not learned how to be a responsible enough mother to support 5 children on her own. Once I received the understanding about her relationship with my father, I was then able to release that bondage that was inside of me. I was able to release pride.

This area of pride was a barrier-breaking event in my life. I did not have any excuse to abuse women. Any man who abuses women in any type of way: physically, spiritually, mentally, verbally, financially, etc. and has an excuse for why he did it, is walking in deception. He is fooling himself because he is walking in pride. A faithful man will love, regardless of any past situation. In the book of Matthew 22:39 'and the second is like unto, Thou shalt love thy neighbor as thyself'.

The people we come in contact with on a daily basis are our neighbors. The Lord says we should treat them the same way we should treat ourselves. People really do not want to hurt or abuse themselves, so why do we do these things to other people?

In Romans 2:11 'for there is no respect of persons with God'. We should treat all people the same. We should give the same respect to our spouses, our children, our parents and even our associates. When we disrespect people, we disrespect God. Jesus said the things that we do to the least of his brethren, we have done it also unto Him. Instead of being mad at people, we should begin to walk in love and forgiveness. Do not throw a hand at someone but 'greet all the brethren with a holy kiss' (1Thessalonians 5:26).

We should free ourselves from this pride, especially men. Some men are too 'macho' to show love to another man. They have a hard time telling each other that God loves them or to say they love each other just as if they were brothers.

In Genesis 4:9-12 the Lord questioned Cain about Abel's whereabouts. Cain responded 'I know not: Am I my brother's keeper'? Cain, who killed his brother, was cursed and punished by God until Cain even said that it was more than he could bear. He had his brother's blood on his hand. Men, we have an assignment to be our brother's keeper. We are all brothers and sisters in Christ.

Do you know where your covenant brothers are? If any harm comes upon our brothers, will their blood be upon your hands? God said we would be responsible if we allow our brothers to suffer any hurt, harm or danger, when it is in our power to stop it. We are our brother's keeper! When we see our brothers, do not be too prideful to give them a hug. Greet them in love because we care about their well-being.

Men tend to allow pride to stop them from expressing any type of love. Let's stop this violent behavior and let's begin to love one another. In Mark 11:25 'when you have aught or when you are mad at one another, you should forgive'. Now, based on the word of God, this is what we should always do.

I personally thought I had all the reasons and excuses to hold grudges, to drink or to mistreat people; however, I was not faithful to the word of God. Regardless of the reason I formulated, I still was not faithful to God. I was not faithful to my mother or my father. I was not faithful in relationships. I could always come up with a reason why I did those things, but the bottom line was that I was not faithful.

God forbid, but if people do not drop this area of pride in their life, then we may see thousands of people on their way to hell telling God why they did the things they did. At this time it will be too late. What they don't realize is that heaven is not going to waste time sorting through all of their excuses. God is only going to judge them based on that which he called them to do. Did you do what God told you to do? Were you faithful to God? Did you forgive your brother? Did you love your mother? Were you your brother's keeper? Did you do unto others, as you would have others do unto you? Did you go to bed mad?

This is what God will look at and not the excuse you have. Do not let pride fool you. Do not allow pride to trick you or deceive you into justifying your wrong actions by giving excuses. 'The fear of the Lord is to hate evil: pride, and arrogancy, and the evil way, and the froward mouth, do I hate' (Proverbs 8:13). When we fear the Lord, we will hate what He hates and love what He loves.

In John 15:12-13 'This is my commandment, that ye love one another, as I have loved you. Greater love hath no man than this, that a man lay down his life for his friends'. This is a true test of love. I realize that it takes the same amount of faith to get mad and hold a grudge against someone as it does to forgive and to forget. Also in the Amplified bible, 1 Peter 4:8 'And above all things have intense and unfailing love for one another, for love covers a multitude of sins (forgives and disregards the offenses of others'). 'Hatred stirreth up strife: but love covereth all sins' (Proverbs 10:12). It is so much easier to love than it is to hate. I thank the Lord for allowing me to love my mother and my family. I love you, mama.

A quick test of pride is this: Are you the type of person who always gives excuses? Do you always have a good explanation to give? Are you always telling people "this is the reason why you did this or that"? Do you always need to explain yourself for something you did? If so, in the name of Jesus I bind that spirit of pride.

I bind that spirit of deception. I cast it out in the name of Jesus. I declare that you walk as a man or woman of God. I declare that you walk in integrity. I pray that you drop this form of pride, drop the excuses and accept your responsibilities for your own actions. Walk by faith and not by sight. You are faithful to God. No weapon formed against you shall prosper. The joy of the Lord is your strength. I declare that you walk in peace, love and humility. Nobody but Jesus Christ sits on the throne of your life. You are faithful to God; therefore, you will always be faithful to your mother and father. You will always be faithful to your wife and children. You will always be faithful to your loved ones, friends and family. In the name of Jesus Christ, the anointed one and his anointing I pray, Amen!

Chapter 12

The choice....confused

I have heard many people say that they cannot let go of pride. It is not always that we can't, but most times we don't drop pride because we don't want to. Excuses that I hear people use all the time to 'justify' their actions is this: "I can't help it". "That is just the way I am". They may say: "I always do that". "It is a habit I have". "That's just me". "You'll need to overlook me". Now, my question to them is this: Is that how God made you? What would Jesus do if He were in your situation? To me, an excuse is only a pathway or an avenue for someone to avoid being faithful or to avoid keeping a promise.

An excuse is like having an escape so that the blame would be put on another person or on the situation. Every time I hear someone constantly giving an excuse for something that they did or did not do, the word pride instantly comes up in my spirit. Remember, in the middle of the word pride is "I".

Excuses are mainly used to protect you and you only. In Deuteronomy 30:19 'I call heaven and earth to record this day against you, that I have set before you life and death, blessing and cursing:

therefore choose life, that both thou and thy seed may live'. In every situation we face in life, we have a choice. In this scripture, the Lord even gives us a hint by telling us to choose life.

When a person does not choose, it is mainly because they are looking for an excuse. However, when you do not choose life, you have automatically chosen death. If you are not going forward then you are backsliding. Sure, people can say that they can't drop their pride. They may say that they can't forgive, they can't love or they can't be a blessing to someone. They may even have valid reasons to justify why they feel that way. However, based on Deuteronomy 30:19 they still have a choice; they still have a decision to make. As I stated earlier, I still feel that it's not always that we can't drop pride, but it's because we don't want to.

I remember working with a young man, who when he came to work, was dressed just like he came out of a fashion magazine. (At times, I can be a pretty 'snappy' dresser myself.) However, this young man was just exceptionally sharp. He seemed to have this unique way that he coordinated his clothes. Well, one day I made this statement to him: "I'll never be able to dress like you do". His response was "If you want to dress like this, you can". Basically, he told me that it was not that I couldn't, but once I made a decision in my mind to change the way I dress, then I could dress anyway that I pleased. If I started to save money, invest, sacrifice or do whatever needed to be done, to improve my wardrobe, then I too could dress the exquisite and immaculate way.

In Matthew 13:15 Jesus said 'For this people's heart is waxed gross, and their ears are dull of hearing, and their eyes they have closed; lest at any time they should see with their eyes, and hear with their ears, and should understand with their heart, and should be converted, and I should heal them'. The choice or decision that we make to change any situation in our lives starts from within our heart. Once you can hear, see and understand in your heart, change can begin. Simply put, anytime that you want to change your life and drop your pride, you have a choice!

Remember, if you still feel like you need help, Jesus has enough anointing to add to your faith and your desire to change, that will propel you to do anything that people said could not be done. It does not take a big miracle or revelation for a person to change, but all it takes is for them to make a quality decision. This decision begins with changing the way that you think.

In Romans 12:2 'and be not conformed to this world: but be ye transformed by the renewing of your mind'. We have to renew our minds. We cannot continue to give excuses. Excuses are just an easy way of conforming to the world's system. As long as we continue to think the same way, then we will always make the same choices. Our bodies will only do and say what is in our minds. If my mind tells me: 'I can't change the way that I dress', my body will dress the same. When a person makes a decision to change, on the inside first, this will start the change process on the outside.

One common factor that I noticed in both Matthew 13 and Romans 12 is how suddenly things happen once you make a choice. ANYTIME you want to change, you can. It does not take a person to go through counseling for weeks, months or years, but at the exact moment you decide to change, the supernatural power of God will move quickly and suddenly. Any excuse we use to justify our inability to change is laziness and slothfulness. They are just too lazy and too slothful to change.

A prideful person can actually be lazy. In Galatians 6:9 'and let us not be weary in well doing: for in due season we shall reap, if we faint not'. Most of the fainting is in the mind. When we drop pride, it begins in the area of the mind. Oh sure, an excuse may be the easy way out, but are you looking for a 'quick fix' or a lifetime of change?

The longer we take to change, the worse the problem will become. Excuses allow us to 'buy' time until we can formulate a justifiable answer to a situation. This will lead you into an area of procrastination. If you do not know what to do, the bible says to ask. Asking allows the love of God to flow through you. Asking is not a sign of ignorance, but it is an indication of a person's desire to learn. It is not dumb to ask questions because the only dumb question to me is one that you don't ask.

Never assume, but go to God when you have questions about how to decide or what to decide. Assumption is the very lowest form of knowledge. In James 1:5 'if any of you lack wisdom, let him ask of God, that giveth to all men liberally, and upbraideth not: and it shall be given him'. So, if you do not know what to do, ask God and he said he would give you what you asked for. Now, continuing in James 1:6 'But let him ask in faith, nothing wavering. For he that wavereth is like a wave of the sea driven with the wind and tossed'.

When you ask, make sure that you have a solid foundation. Make sure you strongly believe in what you are asking for and at the same time, believe in your heart that God will answer you. Furthermore, in James 1:7-8 'For let not that man think that he shall receive any thing of the Lord. A double minded man is unstable in all his ways'. Here, the Lord warns us that if you don't believe that you have received, then do not expect to receive anything. The Lord says that you are double minded or you think twice about situations. He said that a double-minded person changes a lot. They waver, hesitate, doubt and are unreliable and uncertain about their decisions. When you make a choice in life, based on your own emotions and feelings, then yes, you will waver. What will be your foundation?

Your choices in life should be based on what the bible says. In Colossians 3:15 'and let the peace of God rule in your hearts, to the which also ye are called in one body; and be ye thankful'. In the Amplified bible it reads 'and let the peace (soul harmony which comes) from Christ rule (act as umpire continually) in your hearts (deciding and settling with finality all questions that arise in your minds, in that peaceful state) to which as (members of Christ's) one body you were also called (to live). And be thankful (appreciative), (giving praise to God always)'. How can you tell when you made the right decision? You will have the peace of God in your heart, peace in your mind and peace in your life.

What is the peace of God? In the Greek, the word peace means eirene or prosperity, oneness, quietness and rest. There is prosperity in making choices based on the word of God. There is oneness, in which you begin to learn and discover yourself, and who you are in Christ. There is quietness and rest in which you will not have anything to worry about. Nothing will be out of place; nothing will be lacking; nothing will be missing; nothing will be broken; you will be complete in Christ. Drop pride and let the peace of God rule in your hearts just like an umpire rules a game.

Chapter 13

Too close to the door... procrastination

I once watched a television sitcom in which a young lady was giving the love of her life an ultimatum. "Either love me or leave me," she said. She had taken enough of waiting to see when she could say that she was in a committed relationship with a man that hopefully, she would marry one day. After arguing back and forth, she decided to leave and walk out the door. The last words she spoke to him were "If you let me walk out this door, then I'm never coming back". She turned, walked towards the door and began to reach for the doorknob. The man spoke suddenly, "Wait, don't leave. I love you"! After meditating for a moment, she calmly replied: "You should not have let me get this far". In her spirit, if this man had truly known what he wanted, it should not have taken him so long to decide.

This situation should not have gone down to 'love me or leave me'. When you know what you need or what want, there should not be any contemplating or double mindedness. Apparently, this man was not 110% positive if this was the woman he wanted to marry. When you put things off to a later date or time, this is known as procrastination.

This spirit of procrastination robs so many people of so many opportunities. This spirit has a lot to do with pride. If this man had gotten his pride out the way, he would not have waited until the last minute before he spoke what was in his heart. He would have known what he wanted.

Pride does not like being wrong. Pride does not like to make mistakes. Pride has to have the upper hand. If pride is in the way, you tend to think twice about making decisions, mainly because of the affect it might have on your image.

Now, there is nothing wrong with reasoning and being sure you are not making mistakes through quick, impulse actions. There is nothing wrong with making good, rational business decisions. However, if you have come to the point where you have peace in your heart, but you still procrastinate, then pride is creeping in. Pride will still develop excuses because the situation may involve giving up something for someone else. This is one way that pride can cause you to procrastinate.

Pride will make you think about what you will lose. In the above story, this man was worried about losing his freedom. There was no doubt that this woman would make someone a very joyful wife; however, she was also looking for commitment. Commitment meant that there would be some sacrificing that would have to take place.

Pride does not believe in sacrifice. In Proverbs 20:4 'the sluggard will not plow by reason of the cold; therefore shall he beg in harvest, and have nothing'. This farmer was too lazy to plant seed because it was too cold outside. It was not convenient, so he chose to wait. However, when it came time to eat, he reaped what he sowed, which was nothing.

We can come up with all types of excuses for why we wait and put things off, but in reality that's all they are: excuses. We will regret our delayed actions. We should plant seeds now for what we want in the future. When we pray for healing, we should confess now that we are the healed protecting our health. Do not wait until sickness comes over your body, but start declaring your healing now!

In Isaiah 11:2-3 'and the spirit of the Lord shall rest upon him, the spirit of wisdom and understanding, the spirit of counsel and might, the spirit of knowledge and of the fear of the Lord; and shall make him of quick understanding in the fear of the Lord'. When the spirit of the Lord is upon you, you will have a quick understanding. You will not have to think long and hard but your spirit will move quickly and suddenly. This is one reason how pride and procrastination can come into a person's life. When you are not walking in the fear of the Lord or out of reverential respect for God, then you are out of His will.

God speaks to us through our spirit. If our spirit is not in tune with God, then how can we hear Him? If we cannot hear God, then how will our spirit know what to do? Procrastination is that interim time a person goes through when he is trying to figure out what to do. He is confused because he cannot hear from God. It is not until after he drops that spirit of pride and humbles himself before God, that he will be able to hear the wisdom of God and to hear instructions from God. The spirit man is waiting to hear from God, so he can relay the message to the soul, in order for the body to move. The body is not moving because it has not heard from the mind, which has not heard from the spirit. You cannot hear in the spirit realm unless you are walking in the fear of the Lord.

Now, 'on the other side of the stick', the same way that God speaks to us through our spirit, the devil speaks to us through our mind. In John 10:10 'the thief cometh not, but for to steal, and to kill, and to destroy: I am come that they might have life, and that they might have it more abundantly'. If you are not receiving the wisdom of God through your spirit then you are subject to receive the evilness of the devil. Do not forget that you have to make a choice.

Procrastination comes as a result of being out of the presence of God. Procrastination is disobedience. Delayed obedience is also disobedience. When you are walking by faith and living by faith, then the spirit of God will be moving quickly and suddenly through you. The spirit of God is not a lazy procrastinator. The spirit of God is always directed and knows what to do. The spirit of God is not double-minded or indecisive, but it knows His purpose.

In Isaiah 55:11 'so shall my word be that goeth forth out of my mouth: it shall not return unto me void, but it shall accomplish that which I please, and it shall prosper in the thing whereto I sent it'. The word of God will do exactly what it is directed to do. No excuses, no exceptions and no procrastination.

The Holy Spirit will help us decide and will intercede for us. In Romans 8:27 'and he that searcheth the hearts knoweth what is the mind of the Spirit, because he maketh intercession for the saints according to the will of God'. God knows what is in our spirit. Once our spirit is renewed and enlightened, we will then be able to avoid procrastination due to ignorance or by not knowing what to do. The Holy Spirit will lead us and guide us when we allow Him to flow through us.

Pride will draw you away from the will of God. This is another reason why pride is so destructive. Pride will not allow you to walk in the spirit, which will continue to cause delay in hearing from God. This will increase procrastination.

Now, what about the ones who know what to do and still wait and put things off. Many times, we have the answer sitting right in front of our faces, but we are too lazy to lay hold on it. In the book of 2 Peter 2:21-22 'for it had been better for them not to have known the way of righteousness, than, after they have known it, to turn from the holy commandment delivered unto them. But it is happened unto them according to the true proverb, the dog is turned to his own vomit again; and the sow that was washed to her wallowing in the mire'. That sounds ugly, but sometimes the truth is not a very pretty sight. The Lord said, for those of you who know right from wrong; for those who know what to do, when to do it and how, but procrastinate and refuse to act out on the word of God, He called you a dog. Not only a dog, but also a dog that indulges in its own vomit.

We miss so much when we do not follow our heart. However, be careful not to confuse our emotional, impulse reactions with our spirit. You can tell the difference when there is peace in our heart.

The spirit of the Lord is pouring out His blessings continually, but we sometimes wait until the last minute to receive them. Imagine how peaceful life will be when things are done decently and in order. I personally did not like to rush. I did not like standing in line at the post office at 11:59 P.M. trying to get an envelope (that contained a past due bill) date stamped in order to avoid late fees. I didn't like cramming for a test because I waited until the last minute to study.

We miss out on so many opportunities when we don't listen to our spirit man. I used to delay and put things off because of uncertainty in my mind. My pride was a little different than normal in this area of procrastination. In my mind, I had a humbling, prideful spirit; however, in reality I was deceitful and sneaky.

My pride was more concerned with being rejected by people, so I would wait until certain situations 'worked themselves out'. Here is an example. I remember one day in which I drastically needed a day off. All I had to do was to ask my boss for a day off from work. Sounds simple, right? Well, it wasn't. Pride began to remind me that I had already taken a day off last week and that my boss would not grant me another one off so soon. What would happen if my boss said no? How will they feel or how would I feel? One other person may already be off that day. I contemplated all types of different ways just to ask my boss for a day off. Although, I knew in my spirit that I had a very legitimate reason to request the vacation time, pride played with my mind, almost until it was too late. I ended up waiting until it was almost time to get off work the day before I needed to be off.

This example may seem small to some people. Besides, all I had to do was to ask for a day off. If I had not asked my boss, then the destruction would have started. The guilt of not asking would have set in. I would have missed my appointment. I eventually would have needed to rearrange my work and home schedule because my appointment still would have been unresolved.

There are so many people in this world that struggle with this fear of rejection. It is a form of pride that exalts you to a lower status. The longer your mind is trying to formulate the right words to say procrastination is constantly building up. I once saw a newspaper article entitled "Procrastination-the thief of time". Time is valuable, and the enemy wants to steal all of it. So, the devil started this spirit of pride known as procrastination to slow things up.

The world as we know it will soon be over and devils are trembling. They know that in 1 Corinthians 15:52-54 'in a moment, in a twinkling of an eye, at the last trump: for the trumpet shall sound, and the dead shall be raised incorruptible, and we shall be changed'. How shall we be changed? 'For this corruptible must put on incorruption, and this mortal must put on immortality. So when this corruptible shall have put on incorruption, and this mortal shall have put on immortality, then shall be brought to pass the saying that is written, Death is swallowed up in victory'. What does all this mean? JESUS has returned! Hallelujah, hallelujah!

Chapter 14

Directed or Driven?...rejection

Asking God for direction is a very vital part of our Christian walk. Do we truly ask God for daily guidance? Do we truly acknowledge God in all the things that we do? Does God direct us or are we driven by our emotions? In Psalm 19:14 'let the words of my mouth and the meditation of my heart be acceptable in Your sight, O Lord, my strength, and my redeemer'. Are the things that you say or think acceptable in the sight of God? Not only after we say or think something, but also even before we speak; before we think; and before we meditate, have we received God's approval? Has God accepted those words or thoughts? Before we can accept anything, something has to be offered. In this scripture, we need to offer our words and thoughts as a proposal to God and ask if they are okay or acceptable to Him.

Can you truly say that you have asked God for approval and acceptance in every area and every decision of your life? So many times we think or say things and then ask God afterwards: 'Was that acceptable'? It's too late then. You have already done it. You've committed the act before asking God if it was okay. In a sense, this can be related to tempting God. It is almost similar to someone jumping off a bridge and then saying 'Lord send your angels to catch me'. This is simply an already pre-determined decision. In this case, the law of gravity will be in place because of seedtime and harvest.

When we cease to ask God for direction, we are walking in pride. How? Pride is selfish and arrogant. Pride is a resistant force that does not have the intelligence to ask for approval before it reacts. In the middle of pride is "I" so "I" will be the first person that pride will ask for direction from. Pride already thinks it knows it all, so why ask God or why ask anyone else for that matter.

In Proverbs 3:5-6 'trust in the Lord with all thine heart; and lean not unto thine own understanding. In all thy ways acknowledge him, and he shall direct thy paths'. We should trust or have confidence in the Lord because he knows us better than we know ourselves. God created the heaven and the earth. God knows all things. It sounds to me that a person with common sense should not have a problem trusting in the Lord.

Now, I am not saying that you should not have faith in your own ability to make a decision. However, your decisions should be based on the word of God. Doing things based on the word of God means that you are trusting in the Lord. You cannot trust in the Lord and rely on your own understanding at the same time. Your understanding comes from the outside; however, trust comes from the inside. We understand things that we have experienced in the natural. We understand when things are told to us, explained to us or given to us. In order to understand something, you must do it first to learn how it operates.

Trust, on the other hand, is an inward emotion. Trust comes from within your spirit. We are made in the image of God. God is a spirit, and thus, we are spirit beings. When we have trust, we are actually relying on God because of our spirit. Our spirit or our inward man is seeking direction from God when we have trust in Him. When we lean on our own understanding, our mind is seeking direction from outside experiences. Do we trust God or do we trust mankind and its experiences? Now, how do we acknowledge God?

We acknowledge God when we ask Him for direction and guidance. We acknowledge God by allowing Him to become a part of our everyday lives. When your own child asks you for help, how does it make you feel? How does your mind react when they ask you for understanding? I know it makes you feel good. When they ask you a question, this is a clear indication of their love for you and the trust that they have in the things you say. It makes you feel appreciated. It makes you feel confident in your own ability since your own child chose to ask you instead of a friend, a teacher or any other person.

If your child asks your neighbor how to do something instead of asking you, how does that make you feel? Admit it, you probably feel like your child does not trust you. You feel like they love someone else more than they love you. You may feel rejected, betrayed and even hurt. You are supposed to be their parent. You are the one that has a covenant with them, yet and still your covenant child has disrespected you, violated the covenant and chose to seek guidance from someone that does not have the same bond with you.

I know this may sound a little deep, but have you ever thought how God feels when you do not acknowledge Him. How does God feel when we are always seeking counseling from friends, support groups or even psychic lines? God is the one who supplies all of our needs. God is the one who gives us life, health and strength. God is the one who made us. You mean to say that you will choose to seek direction from someone that knows nothing about you rather than to go back to our creator? When we have concerns about our automobile, we would not go to a

Ford dealer to ask questions about a Honda. We would or should go to the manufacturer.

When we do not acknowledge God, we grieve the Holy Spirit. The Holy Spirit is a helper, but how can He help if our backs are turned? How can he help if we are not in a position to receive? Pride will turn you away from the will of God and put your attention on yourself. If you don't acknowledge God then you are acknowledging yourself. If you are not asking God for direction, then someone or something else has become the head of your life.

In Matthew 10:33 'but whosoever shall deny me before men, him will I also deny before my Father which is in heaven'. Most times when we think of denying something or someone, we think about keeping things away from them, holding back or disowning. Deny also means not to acknowledge. This is a sin. There are sins of commission as well as sins of omission. We sin by committing a wrong act or deed outside of the will of God. We also sin by omitting or by not doing the will of God. So, when we deny God, it means we did not acknowledge God.

There are other ways we do not acknowledge God. One way is when we have completed a great accomplishment but don't acknowledge or give God the praise and glory. We do not include or recognize God's presence. We must always remember to acknowledge God by acknowledging the presence of the Holy Spirit. If we begin to take credit for our own success, instead of realizing that God gave us the strength, then we are operating in pride. We must remember that the only way that we can do all things is through Christ, which strengthened us (Philippians 4:13). If we don't acknowledge God then we have denied him. We have denied God's right to show his presence.

We have an assignment from God to restore the earth. The sin of Adam and Eve in the garden turned the world over to Satan, who has been the temporary god of this world's system. If people continue to deny God by not acknowledging him, they will allow Satan to remain in this world. God raised Jesus from the dead for our sins so that we may have a right to the tree of life. In Psalm 24:1 'the earth is the Lord's and the fullness thereof; the world, and they that dwell therein'. This earth and this world belong to God and not Satan.

We must recognize the true source of our strength, which comes only from God. If a person is not trusting in God then they are trusting in the world's system. They are trusting in Satan.

In Deuteronomy 8:17-18 'and thou say in thine heart, My power and the might of mine hand hath gotten me this wealth. But thou shalt remember the Lord thy God: for it is he that giveth thee power to get wealth, that he may establish his covenant which he sware unto thy fathers, as it is this day'. Don't forget God and everything he has done for you. His purpose for giving you the power to get wealth and all the material blessings is to fulfill the covenant promise he made with Abraham in the book of Genesis 17. Abraham would be the father of many nations (verse 4). The covenant was between God, Abraham and his seed after him in their generations. This was an everlasting covenant (verse 7). We are blessed to be a blessing until all families of the earth have been blessed. It is very important to recognize the true source and power of our deliverance, which comes from God only.

We can also deny or not acknowledge God in our everyday conversations with people. Many Christians are in so much bondage to people because of pride. This pride sets in fear of what people will think about them. They are concerned with how they will be received or treated if people find out they are saved, born again, and filled with the Holy

Ghost. You want to know how you'll be treated? You will be persecuted! However, the persecution is for Jesus Christ and not for you. Satan is trying to stop the children of God from laying a hold on what belongs to God, so the devil is running rapid.

Forgive me for sounding harsh, but whether or not you feel you will be persecuted is still not an excuse to not acknowledge God. People may have thousands of reasons for why they did not acknowledge God, but the bottom line is they didn't. They were not faithful to God.

I remember when I was in high school, I was proud to be called 'David Wells' brother. He was the Most Valuable Player on the Griffin High School baseball team. He played for Middle Georgia Jr. College when they won the National Championship. David was like a star in Griffin. Now, here I am with an opportunity to carry on the Wells name, which I did. I was an honor graduate, a good basketball and baseball player and was voted most likely to succeed by my peers. I always told people that my brother and my daddy taught me a lot. They instilled values, proper home training and a strong desire in me to succeed. I acknowledged that the talents I operated in were because of what I learned from them.

Now, the exact same way that I acknowledged my brother and daddy should be the same way we acknowledge God. We should remember to thank God for all that he has done for and for us and thank God for all that he is doing in our lives. Why is it that we can put so much trust and acknowledgement in man but not in God? It is easy to have faith in those people or things that we can see, however, those things are only temporary. We should put our trust in our eternal God.

Today, I am free from people bondage. I am free from pride that once stopped me from raising my hands and saying "hallelujah". "Thank you

Jesus"! Pride stopped me from giving praise and worship to God. Pride stopped the tears from rolling down my cheek when I began to reverence God. Pride stopped me from going to the altar to bow down on my knees before God. Pride stopped me from praying in tongues. Pride stopped me from tithing. Pride stopped me from fasting. Pride stopped me from acknowledging the presence of the Holy Spirit. Pride had me rejecting God.

Thank you Jesus that today I am free. 'I am not ashamed of the gospel of Jesus Christ: for it is the power of God unto salvation to every one that believeth' (Romans 1:16). God is not ashamed of us. In Hebrews 11:16 'wherefore God is not ashamed to be called their God'. God rejoices when he is called our God. 'Beloved, I wish above all things that thou mayest prosper and be in health, even as thy soul prospereth' (3 John 1:2). 'Let them shout for joy, and be glad, that favour my righteous cause: yea, let them say continually, Let the Lord be magnified, which hath pleasure in the prosperity of his servant' (Psalm 35:27).

It gives God joy to know that He is our God and we are His people. So, why be ashamed to admit that God is our Father and we are the children of God? If we can recognize our natural parents, we should also recognize and acknowledge our spiritual parent, our heavenly Father-God Almighty!

This is why it is so important to acknowledge God first. We must ask God for direction, so he can direct our paths. We must be directed by God and led by God to give, to bless others, to speak, to walk and to move. The Holy Spirit must direct us. He is our guide. He is our path of righteousness. In Psalm 37:23 'the steps of a good man are ordered by the Lord: and he delighteth in his way'. The Amplified version says 'the steps of a (good) man are directed and established by the Lord when He delights in his way (and He busies Himself with his every step)'.

The Lord enjoys directing our path because it gives him pleasure with each step and each decision that we make. God is the one who sets things in order. God gives the command. Why? God is the Alpha and the Omega, the beginning and the end. He knows what lies ahead of us and what is behind us. We look at the weather channel to determine how we should prepare for each day. If the weather report predicts rain, we will take an umbrella or if there will be cold weather, we take a coat.

Now, when we do not acknowledge God so He can direct our path, we risk being driven by pride. Pride is a force that will draw you away from the will of God and drive you towards the things of the world. Before you do anything else, ask yourself this question: "Am I directed by God or am I driven by my emotions"? When you are driven, your spirit feels resistance, uneasiness and confusion. The Holy Spirit is a gentleman. He is kind and considerate. The Holy Spirit is peaceful. Contrary, pride is selfish. Pride is concerned with getting even. Pride stirs up strife, confusion, anger and turmoil.

This is one way to tell if you are directed by God or driven by your emotions. Is there peace? I once heard this cliché: "You can control your actions or reactions, but you cannot control someone else's actions or reactions". When we act or react to a situation or when we allow a situation to change the way we would normally think or feel, then we are being driven. We are driven because we did not acknowledge God. We are then conforming to those circumstances.

Did God give us permission to act that way or was it our own decision? Did we give God the glory for the decision we made? Was our decision acceptable to God? Were we proud that God was a part of our decision? These are questions to determine whether or not you are directed by God or driven by your emotions. We always have a choice. Will you choose to acknowledge God?

Chapter 15

The Tower of Babylon...loneliness

Accomplishments in life are the results of intense, dedicated and consistent actions. A lot of work was put forth in their achievements, and now it is graduation time. Now it is time to receive the reward for the end of their faith. The emotion a person feels for accomplishing a task that seemed almost unattainable is just wonderful. They feel proud of themselves because through their efforts, the impossible was made possible. However, based on the vision and purpose the individual operated in before and after obtaining this accomplishment, will determine whether or not they were in pride.

The story of the Tower of Babylon is one such example. In Genesis 11:1-9 a nation of people (descendants of Noah, Shem, Ham, and Japheth in Genesis 10) went on a journey to find a new place to live. They found a land in Shinar in which they dwelt there. They all spoke the same language, had the same speech and were all on one accord. They all were in agreement with one another and they all worked together.

Now, think with me for a moment. Today it is hard to get two people to come together: let alone a whole nation of people. Imagine the power that has been made available through the power of agreement. In Matthew 18:19-20 Jesus said that 'if two or three people come together, in His name, then He will be in the midst of us and will give us anything that we ask'. There are blessings in the power of agreement. You will never be alone as long as you are walking in agreement.

This nation of Shinar appeared to be moving in the right direction. There was one problem. Even though the people of Shinar were together, they were not single. You might ask: "well, Brother Wells, I thought the purpose of them coming together was so they would not be single". "Since they are in agreement then they can't be single, so what is the problem"? Good question.

First, you have to understand what it means to be single. Single means more than just to be alone or isolated. One definition of single is to be exclusive, sole, unique, separate, rare, complete or different. Single means to have your own identity. It means to be entire or whole where there is nothing missing. You still might ask: "well, Brother Wells, God did not seem to have a problem with people being together because in Genesis 2:18 He said 'It is not good that man should be alone'. Yes, God did say it was not good to be alone, but did He have a problem with a person being single?

Whether we realize it or not, we are all single. You can be married but single at the same time. We all have unique and separate features about ourselves. Out of the billions of people in this world, no two people have the same fingerprints. God created us this way, so apparently he has no problem with singleness. We should be single, unique individuals with our own personalities and our own way of thinking. We should be distinct, rare and complete. We should have everything together: spirit, soul, and body.

The people of Shinar were once single. In Genesis 10:5 they were '...in their own lands, each with his own language, by their families within their nation'. This was a sign of singleness because there were different lands, languages, families and nations.

What makes being different a benefit? This is how. When you take two single, unique individuals and give them the same vision, the task will be completed; however, it will include each individual's singleness. Since they have the same vision, the goal will still be accomplished. Singleness will add the uniqueness to the vision. Alexander Graham Bell invented the telephone. What if everybody, who has made additions to the telephone, was just like Alexander Graham Bell? Every telephone would consist of two cups joined together by a string. But, because local telephone companies added their singleness to Mr. Bell's invention, we now have touch-tone, automatic re-dial, caller-id, call return and other phone features. The telephone still has the same vision and purpose, but now, it is more single.

How does this relate to the Tower of Babylon and the people of Shinar that built it? In Genesis 11:4 they said 'let us build us a city and make a tower, whose top may reach unto heaven..' This is where pride starts to come in. Why did they build the tower? What was their purpose or their vision? Were they building the tower to please God or to please themselves?

One reason they came together was because they were not single anymore. Nobody had any unique, separate or exclusive characteristics about themselves. Nobody had any identity. In continuing with verse 4 '...and let us make us a name, lest we be scattered abroad upon the face of the whole earth'. This was a clear indication of a nation that was about to lose their identity. They wanted to make a name for themselves because of fear. They did not have any confidence in their own ability to stand, to the point, they felt they needed each other to help prevent them from being 'scattered abroad upon the face of the whole earth'. I see a nation full of pride.

First, they were not single. Secondly, they did not include God. Thirdly, they walked in fear and wanted to separate themselves from everybody. They wanted to make themselves a name and to create their own kingdom. They, in actuality, wanted to create their own god. They did not want to associate with other people unless they were a part of the Shinar clique. They wanted to be alone, isolated and governed by their own rules and regulations. They were alone but they were not single. They were a lonely people who felt they needed the presence of others to make them feel complete or that they belonged with others.

Now, let me add balance to this. The people of Shinar had the right intention in mind. It was an excellent idea to come together in agreement and build the tower. However, they lacked singleness, vision, purpose but most importantly-God. Their purpose was only to escape the world. There was no real objective in mind. They had a good idea but not a God idea.

Ask yourself a question: Are you trying to build any 'Towers of Babylon' in your life? Are you trying to start a business without God? Are you starting a business for the purpose of financial freedom only or do you want to be blessed with money so you can bless someone else? Are you a member of a church that is trying to separate from the world and from God? Does your church focus on taking care of its members only or are they trying to help change your community, your friends, family and ultimately, the world?

If you are doing ANYTHING that only has a selfish motive, vision, or purpose, you may be building a Tower of Babylon. This nation of Shinar operated in pride because they too were selfish and were only thinking about themselves.

The Lord noticed their work and knew that this pride would only lead them to destruction. In Genesis 11:5-7 'and the Lord came down to see the city and the tower, which the children of men builded. And the Lord said, Behold, the people is one, and they have all one language; and this they begin to do; and now nothing will be restrained from them, which they have imagined to do. Go to, let us go down, and there confound their language, that they may not understand one another's speech'. The Lord had to put a stop to this. There was no idea of what might happen next. 'So the Lord scattered them abroad thence upon the face of all the earth; and they left off to build the city' (Verse 8). Remember in verse 4, the people of Shinar were afraid of being scattered upon the earth. Well, the very thing they feared happening to them was the very thing that destroyed them.

If you let fear enter in your heart, it will set up an avenue for that very thing to haunt you forever. You must learn to submit to God and resist the devil and all his temptations. The people of Shinar were not building the tower in faith but they really were in fear. Fear is the strength of the devil while faith is the strength of God.

Finally, in Genesis 11:9 'therefore is the name of it called Babel; because there the Lord did there confound the language of all the earth: and from thence did the Lord scatter them abroad upon the face of all the earth'. Today we use the word 'babble' when someone is talking continually without making a point or talking excessively without a vision or purpose. I sometimes tell people that gossip a lot that 'I see your lips moving, but you are not saying anything'. Are you babbling and speaking a lot of gibberish, confused language when you talk? If so, search your heart to see if you have built a tower of Babylon.

A Tower of Babylon is formed when a person speaks or does things without understanding or without purpose. In the Amplified bible, 2 Timothy 2:15-16 says 'study and be eager and do your utmost to present yourself to God approved (tested by trial), a workman who has no cause to be ashamed, correctly analyzing and accurately dividing (rightly handling and skillfully teaching) the word of truth. But avoid all empty (vain, useless, idle) talk, for it will lead people into more and more ungodliness'. In other words, don't babble or work without a vision.

There were several things to learn from the story of the Tower of Babylon. First, their vision was not to please God, but to please themselves only. They would have only given themselves credit for their accomplishments instead of acknowledging God or giving God the glory. When we fail to recognize the true source of our help and strength, we are setting ourselves up for judgement. In Matthew 10:32-33 Jesus warns us that 'if we deny Him before men, He will deny us before the Father'. Child of God, do not ever forget that it is God who gives us the strength to accomplish everything in life.

Secondly, this nation had fear before they began to build the city. Remember, in Genesis 11:4, they feared being scattered abroad the face of the earth, which was the ending result in Genesis 11:8. Ironically, the same thing happened to Job. In Job 2:25-26, he feared losing his children, his possessions and his prosperity, and because of this fear, it came upon him as well. The fear that was within him summoned the devil and gave strength to Satan and his evil spirits. Pride is the power twin of fear. Most people who set out to achieve great accomplishments are not always inspired through faith of success but rather from fear of failing.

Thirdly, although there is great strength in the power of agreement, if God is not included then you are still operating in sin. In Romans 14:23 '...for whatsoever is not of faith is sin'. In the book of Matthew 18:19-20 'there must be two or three gathered together in the name of Jesus'. Not one time did the people of Babylon acknowledge God while in the midst of their building. Before you begin to start a business, college, or any other desire of your heart, always place God at the beginning of your journey, during your journey, and after your journey. Once you have completed the journey and accomplished your goal, thank God by giving Him all the praise, all the glory and all the honor.

Fourthly, the people did not have a vision or purpose. In Proverbs 29:18 'where there is no vision, the people perish'. People perish because all of the resources they gathered were wicked since God was not included. When you do not have a vision in line with the will of God, He is unable to provide the provision necessary to bring in His manifestation. His provision supports your vision.

How many Towers of Babylon have we built in our own lives? How many times have we tried to do things without God? Sure, when we get in trouble, we will try to call on God. Why don't we include God in our plans before the trouble? What is your foundation? What is your vision? What are you standing on? We should never tempt God. We should never have the mentality of 'jumping off a building of challenges and temptations' and then start to pray and expect for God to send his angels to catch us. God and his angels should be with us before the challenges, during the challenge and at the end of our faith.

The Tower of Babylon was a story of people coming together in agreement to accomplish a purpose; however, they did not include God as their foundation. The bible tells us that 'faith without works is dead' (James 2:17), but working without faith or working without the word of

God is dead and ineffective also. We should always remember to acknowledge God's presence. We must acknowledge Him by giving Him all the praise and all the glory for everything that we do and for everything that we are.

We need to thank God for our being single, unique, distinctive, complete and whole. Do not allow loneliness to rob you of what God has for you. You do not need any person on this earth to make you feel complete or welcome. We have the Holy Ghost, which Jesus left for us, to comfort us. If you feel lonely, remember that Jesus said He would NEVER leave you nor forsake you. Jesus is right here in your hearts, and regardless of how you feel, He is always with you.

We should never compromise our belief and faith in God by becoming unequally yoked with a situation that we know is not of God. We should never be ashamed to admit that it is God who gives us the strength to live. It is God who wakes us up every morning. It is God who carries us and leads us and guides us. It is God who sends his angels to watch over us and to watch over His word to make sure that the word of God will not return void but will always produce.

Never deny God. Never hold God back. Never keep God out of our plans. Include God in everything. It is His right to be there. 'That, as according as it is written, He that glorieth, let him glory in the Lord' (1 Corinthians 1:31). 'Without God we are nothing, but we can do all things through Christ which strengtheneth us' (Philippians 4:13).

Chapter 16

Promotion cometh from the Lord...arrogance

I once had a conversation with an associate who stated that he was believing God for a promotion. He wanted a better job that would pay him a minimum of $10 per hour. He was determined that he was not going to accept anything less. I was impressed (at first) with the standards he set for his life. Even though $10 per hour may not be a lot to some of you, it almost doubled his current salary, so he was indeed walking by faith.

I then asked him about his present employer and the type of work he was doing now. To my surprise, he was only working part-time temporary assignments through various agencies that paid him an average of $6 per hour. The work was never consistent and some weeks he would only work 3 days. He only worked if he received a phone call or when there was work available. His reason for staying with the temporary agencies was that he was not going to look for or accept a permanent position or any other job elsewhere unless it paid him at least $10 per hour.

Since he only worked about 20 hours per week through the temporary assignments, I told him about a position in the mailroom that was open with my company. The job paid $8 per hour and it was a full-time assignment. The job was also long-term through a temporary agency, which meant he could work there permanently until he was hired or fired.

Normally, all the temporary employees become permanent after a 90-day probationary period. I told him there was also opportunity for advancement and promotion. He could also apply in different departments such as data entry, processing, customer service or research. It depended on his desire to advance. To my surprise, his answer was no.

This man was up to his ears in debt. He only worked about 20 hours per week at his current job making $6 per hour. He had no gas in his car, barely had food to eat and did not even have money to give an offering in church. I proceeded to tell him that "I understand your $10 per hour standard, which will happen at God's appointed time and due season". "But, what if God wanted to see if you could be faithful at a company on a long-term assignment, for a little less money"? "Could you be faithful at $8 per hour before you received your promotion to $10 per hour"? Again, he said no. I was then led by the spirit to sow a financial seed into his life, which he gladly accepted.

I discerned in my spirit that his pride was in the way. His next step may be destruction since there was no steady income coming into his household. His pride made him feel that by accepting less money it meant he would be lowering his standards. The next time I saw him, about three months later, he was not driving but was riding public transportation.

I have not had the opportunity to talk with him about his current situation. All I can do is to continue to pray and intercede for him that God show him grace and mercy until he receive the promotion he has been seeking. Question: Is there anything wrong with this man's attitude? Well, although he was standing on the word of God for promotion, he did not understand the requirement of being a steward. 'A steward is found faithful' (1 Corinthians 4:2). A steward must take care of the things he has now.

Yes, I understand and believe strongly in setting standards, however, I do have a problem with people that allow bills to pile up because of not doing whatever it takes to take care of responsibilities. I have a problem with a man that will refuse to 'get his hands dirty' and do what is necessary in order to take care of his home. Instead, they will choose to keep their nails clean while their life is crumbling before their eyes.

My daddy worked 3 jobs at one time in order to make sure that there was food on our table. My daddy was not too prideful to mop floors, take out trash or clean windows if it meant that his family would be taken care of. Today, so many people have so much pride until it is ridiculous. They have this image to protect. They act as if they are too good to work at certain places. If I have a choice between picking up trash for a paycheck, in order to pay my bills as opposed to sleeping in the trash because my pride would not accept just any job, then let me pick up the trash.

All of my life I have set high goals and standards for my life. At the same time, I realize that there is a progression and growing stage to accomplish these goals. People have to understand that not all blessings will come at one time. Fruit grows in seasons. In Mark 4:26-29 we see the progression stage for the kingdom of God system. When we cast a seed in the ground, the earth will bring forth the fruit: first the blade, then the ear, after that the full corn in the ear.

Just because the person I was trying to help was not immediately offered $10 per hour from my company, did not mean he would not reach that level. At least he was working in the right direction. He really turned down a promotion that God had placed in his life through me. Little did he know that God was sending a blessing to him. I offered $8 per hour and maybe the next person would offer $10, $12 or $15 per hour. He may never know unless he can show his faithfulness in the least. Since he did not receive the immediate promotion to $10, he chose not to accept anything at all.

According to Psalm 75:6-7 'for promotion cometh neither from the east, nor from the west, nor from the south. But God is the judge: he putteth down one, and setteth up another'. His promotion will come from God only. This individual rejected a promotion to $8 per hour and chose to stay at $6 per hour. Now, he may be suffering even more due to a lack of finances. It is not until the past due bills, evictions and repossessions begin to take place, that some people will start praying and believing God. They will then consider this is what it means to have faith. Now, they will decide to wait on the Lord to bless them. The Lord was already blessing them, but they just did not realize it and lay hold on it from the beginning.

Do not ever miss a supernatural blessing from God while looking for a spectacular event. This young man was apparently looking for a spectacular promotion, while God was working supernaturally at His own time and at His own pace. Quite often we can get caught up in our everyday lives by looking for a blessing from God the way that WE want to receive it. God has a million ways to bless us, but all we need is one.

We should never limit God to being able to bless us in just one way. We should never say that if God does not bless me the way that I want to be blessed, then we say it is not from God. Our blessing can come in the mailbox, on the telephone, in the street, in a store, from a friend or family member, through a stranger, through an animal, in the morning, noon, or night, at home, at church or anywhere, anyway or anyhow God wants to get it to you.

Let's go back to Psalm 75:6 'for promotion cometh neither from the east, nor from the west, nor from the south'.

I always wondered why the Lord did not mention the north. The Lord revealed to me that He wants people to know that though promotion may not come from those directions, it might come from an avenue that was not mentioned. It might come in a way that may not be familiar with you. He did not want people to have one-track minds into thinking that they know how and when their promotion would come. He did not mention the north because it was His way of showing us that He has other directions and other ways to bless us.

Let me give you an example. I needed to invest in a computer so I could do the work of the Lord more efficiently and more effectively. I was beginning to write books, poems and inspirational messages revealed to me from God. I wanted to share these revelations with the world. The Lord spoke to me and said that the computer I purchase will be debt free. Did this mean I would walk in a store and the salesman would bless me with a free computer? I did not know how God would bless me. Once I walked in a store, another customer could have blessed me. The Lord could have placed a coupon in my hands. The Lord could have let me be the 1,000th customer in a store's promotional contest. I could have purchased the computer and the Lord would reimburse me later. I could have received a $3,000 check in the mail.

My point is when the Lord spoke and let me know the computer will be debt free, He had millions of ways to bless me. I could not limit my thinking to just 'south, east and west'. 'God is able to exceeding abundantly above all that we ask or think' (Ephesians 3:20). In the Amplified bible, this scripture reads 'Now to Him Who, by (in consequence of) the (action of His) power that is at work within us, is able to (carry out His purpose and) do superabundantly, far over and above all that we (dare) ask or think (infinitely beyond our highest prayers, desires, thoughts, hopes or dreams). God is a big God!

The destructive part of pride is that pride thinks 'it is my way or the highway'. Pride wants to be blessed the way it wants to be blessed, so the eyes of pride are closed. Never limit God's ability to bless you. Do not limit God in your thinking. Do not limit God in your relationships. Do not limit God in His ability to choose the husband or wife that He desires for you to have. Never place God's grace and mercy in a box and give Him only 2 or 3 ways to bless you or never limit yourself to ways that you will receive His blessings. Do not limit God. No more limits! No more limits! No more limits!

We must make sure that our spiritual eyes are wide open. We must be able to discern between that which is good or evil. God can send a blessing in anyway that He chooses. The blessing can come through a child or an adult. The blessing can come through a friend or a stranger. We must put trust in God. Not only should we trust God, we should also trust the people He has placed in our lives: especially the ministers and pastors of your local churches. In 2 Chronicles 20:20 'Believe in the Lord your God, so shall ye be established; believe his prophets, so shall ye prosper'.

Now, what do you do when the Lord blesses you with a promotion? Thank Him! In Deuteronomy 8:17-18 'and thou say in thine heart, My power and the might of mine hand hath gotten me this wealth. But thou shalt remember the Lord thy God: for it is he that giveth thee power to get wealth, that he may establish his covenant which he sware unto thy fathers, as it is this day'. Promotion comes from the Lord. It is not from our intellect or from our ability. We should never say 'I received a promotion'. We should always say 'this is the Lord's doing and it is marvelous in our eyes' (Psalm 118:23).

He promotes us and blesses us in order to be a blessing to someone else. Many people talk about what they have done or what they have accomplished, but in the midst of their blessings, don't forget the Lord. In Matthew 6:33-34 'But seek ye first the kingdom of God, and his righteousness; and all these things shall be added unto you. Take therefore no thought for the morrow: for the morrow shall take thought for the things of itself. Sufficient unto the day is the evil thereof'. 'In God we boast all the day long, and praise thy name for ever' (Psalm 44:8). Without God we are nothing, but we can do all things-through Christ!

Chapter 17

Seedtime and Harvest...
disobedience

'So is the kingdom of God, as if a man should cast seed into the ground; and should sleep, and rise night and day, and the seed should spring and grow up, he knoweth not how. For the earth bringeth forth fruit of herself; first the blade, then the ear, after that the full corn in the ear. But when the fruit is brought forth, immediately he putteth in the sickle, because the harvest is come' (Mark 4:26-29).

I once saw a homeless gentleman walking down the street working very hard. He was pushing a shopping cart while stopping along the way picking up aluminum cans that he would probably sell to make about $5 or $10 dollars. I wondered to myself, 'how did his life change so much that led him to the streets? I asked God: "How could that happen"? He could not have been born that way. I heard a soft voice answer me saying 'seedtime and harvest'.

I have learned through the years that nothing just happens. Our position in life today is a result of the seeds we have sown. This particular gentleman was different than most homeless people I have seen. He did not appear to be the 'begging' type. This man did not look at me. He simply rushed by me as if to say 'I don't need any help'. Then it hit me, that's the problem. He thinks he does not need or want any help from anybody.

It seems as if he was the type who would choose to let his pride stand in the way of him asking for help. He would rather starve, pick up cans in the street or remain homeless rather than let anybody think that he can't get his life back together. With that type of closed mind, it would be very difficult for God to pour his blessings on him. I believe strongly in God's system, which is seedtime and harvest.

Think with me for a moment. If a person spends their life confessing that they do not need or want any help from anyone, should they be surprised if they don't get any help? When you say you don't want anything from anybody, then the law of seedtime and harvest will give you what you asked for—nothing! These types of people can become double-minded so easily. In their hearts, they know that they need and want God to bless them. Yet and still, when God works through people to bless them, they refuse to accept the very thing that they prayed to receive.

In the book of James 1:5-8 'if any of you lack wisdom, let him ask of God, that giveth to all men liberally, and upbraideth not; and it shall be given him. But let him ask in faith, nothing wavering. For he that wavereth is like a wave of the sea driven with the wind and tossed. For let not that man think that he shall receive any thing of the Lord. A double-minded man is unstable in all his way'.

So many people have prayed for wisdom and answers to their problems. God said when you ask, it will be given to us. However, if people ask, when they don't truly believe they will receive, God said this is wavering faith. It is just like the wave of the sea. He said your faith would be tossed around because you will believe anything you see or hear.

When we ask God for anything, we should stand on that prayer in faith until we see the manifestation of what we prayed for. We should not pray and ask God to bless us, and when the blessing comes, we say 'I don't receive it'. I am sure that many people, including the gentleman I saw walking down the street, have asked God to bless them. If God sends someone your way to bless you, then He has answered your prayer. If you do not receive God's blessing then why did you pray? Do you want God to bless you or not?

When your faith in God is 'wavery', God said do not expect to receive anything because you are double-minded. You are double-minded because you are thinking twice about your prayer. Once a person decides what it is they will believe God for, they should stick with it until the end.

In Genesis 8:22 'while the earth remaineth, seedtime and harvest, and cold and heat, and summer and winter, and day and night shall not cease'. God said seedtime and harvest would be here forever. The kingdom of God system is based on seedtime and harvest. We have to understand this principal that everything on the earth works by. In Galatians 6:7 '..whatsoever a man soweth, that shall he also reap'. You will reap what you sow. In this scripture, God lets you know what type of seed a man can sow.

He said 'whatsoever' a man soweth, he will reap. If you sow a money seed, you will reap a money seed. If you sow a food seed, you will reap a food seed. If you sow a word seed, you will reap a word seed. If you sow a doubt and unbelief seed, you will reap a seed of doubt and unbelief. Even if you sow a seed of not doing anything, then you will reap a seed of not doing anything. It does not matter. That is why we must be very sensitive to everything that we look at, everything that we listen to, everything that we say, every place that we go and everything that we do. God said that 'whatsoever' you sow you will reap.

Negative thoughts are seeds. Friendliness is a seed. Anger is a seed. Fear is a seed. We must come to the point by which we judge our lives daily. We must live our life as if our life was a seed. The devil will try to trick your mind into thinking that looking at sin will not hurt as long as you are not committing the act. For so long, we have been told we must physically do something in order to sow a seed. You must also realize that when you do not sow, you do not reap. If you are not sowing a seed, somebody is. In John 10:10 'the thief cometh not, but for to steal, and to kill, and to destroy: I am come that they might have life, and that they might have it more abundantly'. We are in a spiritual warfare. The devil is trying to kill us, however, God, through his son Jesus, is trying to give us life.

There are many types of seeds. However, one type of seed, which is one of the most powerful seeds, is words. God created the world with words. People use words so casually as if they have no effect or no real meaning at all. We say things or ask for things without thinking. We should be careful what we ask for because we might just get it.

We say things such as 'he makes me sick'. 'She gets on my nerves'. 'I almost died laughing at that joke'. We condemn people with our words when we tell them 'to go to hell'. Do we realize what we are saying? We fail to realize that the words we speak will produce what we say.

God needs words of faith to produce his manifestation in our lives. The devil operates the same way by using words of fear, doubt and unbelief to produce his evilness in our lives. It is very dangerous, for a person who walks in pride, to speak. Pride will say: "I don't want any help". "I can do it by myself". "Leave me alone". If those word seeds are not rebuked, they will produce everything that was said. So, do not be surprised.

It is imperative that we be careful of the words that we let come out of our mouths. As I said earlier, I strongly believe that nothing 'just happens'. I believe that at one point in time, a seed was sown and a harvest was reaped. Some seeds may grow instantly while others may take years to grow. We may look at a homeless person today and feel sorry for him, but I guarantee that if you looked at the root of his problem, you will see a bad seed that was sown. 'Be not deceived; God is not mocked: for whatsoever a man soweth, that shall he also reap' (Galatians 6:7). 'But seek ye first the kingdom of God, and his righteousness; and all these things shall be added unto you' (Matthew 6:33).

Chapter 18

Tithing….unbelief

Just like the love of money if the root to all evil, so is pride the root to destruction. The love of money will keep a person from giving. The love of money will make a person think that they are losing out or decreasing every time money leaves their hands. They want to hold on to money as if it was their life. They cannot see themselves blessing another person, especially a church, because they need to know for a certainty that 'their' money will return to them. This is one reason why some people have a problem with tithing. They only see tithing as giving 'their' money away to a church. They do not see tithing as you giving back to God what rightfully belongs to Him.

In Malachi 3:7-9 'even from the days of your fathers ye are gone away from mine ordinances, and have not kept them. Return unto me, and I will return unto you, saith the Lord of hosts. But ye said, Wherein shall we return? Will a man rob God? Yet ye have robbed me. But ye say, Wherein have we robbed thee? In tithes and offerings. Ye are cursed with a curse: for ye have robbed me, even this whole nation'.

God is clearly stating that you have not followed his order. He is telling us that we must return the tithes and offerings back to Him. They DO NOT belong to us. They belong to God. If you don't return the tithes and offerings, he called you a God-robber. I would not want to face God on judgement day with the label of 'God-robber' written across my chest. I do not think that would be the right time to wear that shirt.

What do we do with the tithes? 'Bring ye all the tithes into the storehouse, that there may be meat in mine house, and prove me now herewith, saith the Lord of hosts, if I will not open you the windows of heaven, and pour you out a blessing, that there shall not be room enough to receive it' (Malachi 3:10). Interesting, isn't it? God said if you return the tithes that already belong to Him he will reward you for it. Think about it for a minute in the natural. Would you reward someone that returned money back that belonged to you?

So many people look at tithing as losing, when in actuality, it really does not even belong to us. We are returning the tithes to the 'lost and found' department, and because of our faithfulness, God will open the windows of heaven for us. God is good! Now, the implication is that if you don't tithe, the windows of heaven will be closed and we will be living a sinful, limited life.

Why not tithe? God will reward you for tithing, even though it belongs to Him anyway. Pride will say: "when will I get my reward"? 'O love the Lord, all ye saints: for the Lord preserveth the faithful, and plentifully rewardeth the proud doer' (Psalm 31:23). Pride is really looking for an immediate return. If it is not received when they think they should get it, most likely they will stop and move on to another 'investment' venture. That is the problem. They treat tithing like the world's system. They do not understand the kingdom of God's system.

In Mark 4:26-29 'so is the kingdom of God, as if a man should cast seed into the ground; and should sleep, and rise night and day, and the seed should spring and grow up, he knoweth not how. For the earth bringeth forth fruit of herself; first the blade, then the ear, after that the full corn in the ear. But when the fruit is brought forth, immediately he putteth in the sickle, because the harvest is come'.

The kingdom of God's system is first, something has to be planted in the ground. Next, it tells us to 'sleep, and rise night and day'. In the Greek, sleep means to rest in respect of God; to have intensity; to abide in or to join in. Rise means to arise from sleep; to stand or rear up in expectation, or to change your posture and your position. After you have cast the seed in the ground you must expect it to grow. We expect by reading, confessing and meditating on the word of God. We should be patient, remaining the same while waiting and expecting God to produce the manifestation of the seed we have sown. Sleep does not mean to roll over in our bed and forget about our seed, but sleep means to begin applying faith pressure on the word of God.

Thirdly, the seed should spring and grow. To the natural mind, a person will not know how it grew, but spiritually, we know that God's word will never return void. Fourthly, we must understand how seeds grow. Seeds grow in levels, stages and seasons. Finally, after the growing stage, we can put in the sickle and begin to reap our harvest! So many times, people are looking for a quick fix. The kingdom of God system is seed-time and harvest. We plant our seed, take care of that seed, and give that seed time to grow.

Pride thinks that no matter why, no matter when or no matter how they plant their seeds that it should grow and produce. In Mark 4:3-8, 13-20 it talks about a sower that sowed seed in four different types of ground, but only one produced a harvest. The sower that sowed on good ground was the one that heard the word of God and received it in his heart. They had faith and expectation in God. The word of God was their foundation, which is why the ground they sowed in was good. We must be selective when we sow our seeds.

Are we sowing our seed in ground in which God is the foundation? In addition to the ground we sow in, is the ground of our heart good? How is our heart condition before we sow? What was the purpose for sowing? Do we sow to please ourselves or to please God? Once you realize that tithing is giving back to God what already belongs to Him, then your tithing will be for God and not man. Your heart will have the right condition. I heard someone once say that your heart condition determines your harvest condition. If you sow a seed while your heart is hollow and empty, do not be surprised if your harvest is the same way—hollow and empty.

Tithing is a commandment from God. In Leviticus 27:30, 32 'and all the tithe of the land, whether of the seed of the land, or of the fruit of the tree, is the Lord's: it is holy unto the Lord. The tenth shall be holy'. In the book of Numbers 18:26 '…ye shall offer up an heave offering of it for the Lord, even a tenth part of the tithe'. Also, in Proverbs 3:9 'honour the Lord with thy substance, and with the firstfruits of all thine increase'. We must honor, respect and give God total authority and dominion over the tithe, and also over the first part of all our increase. We must honor the Lord with the tithe.

How are you honoring God? What are you honoring God with? Do you honor God with the firstfruits or with the leftovers after we have taken care of everything else? Whatever we present to the Lord is what we will reap. The amount is not as important as the attitude attached to it. Your attitude will determine your altitude. This will determine how high or how low you will go in life.

Now, let us go back to one of the biggest excuse pride will use for not tithing. They don't physically see or know where their money is going or how it will come back. They do not understand that it takes faith in God to tithe. Faith requires you to believe that you have received before you see it. Your faith is based on the word of God. One thing that people don't realize is 'that whatsoever is not of faith is sin' (Romans 14:23). This means that if a person tithes, but does not have faith, then this is sin. At the same time, a person who does not tithe is living in sin. In Proverbs 13:22 'the wealth of the sinner is laid up for the just'. In Mark 4:25 'for he that hath, to him shall be given: and he that hath not, from him shall be taken even that which he hath'.

The just are the ones who obey God's commandment to tithe. The just are walking by faith. The sinner is actually working for the just. So, a person with pride who does not believe in tithing, will lose his money anyway. According to the word of God, you will give one way or another. You can give so it will be given unto you (Luke 6:38) or you can choose not to give and it will be given to the person that does give.

There are benefits beyond limits in giving. First, I tithe because I am giving back to God and I am obeying His commandment. Secondly, I am storing my resources up in heaven. In Philippians 4:17 '...I desire fruit that may abound to your account'. I sow seeds that are now in my heavenly account. I have an account because I have sown seeds into it. Whenever I have a need, I simply make a withdrawal from my account. Remember, pride will rob you of this rightful inheritance that we have. 'Be not deceived; God is not mocked: whatsoever a man soweth, that shall he also reap' (Galatians 6:7).

Chapter 19

Hindrance to faith....inconsistent

Pride hinders faith. In Hebrews 11:1 'now faith is the substance of things hoped for, the evidence of things not seen'. In Romans 10:17 'faith cometh by hearing and hearing by the word of God'. Faith comes by hearing the word of God. If you do not have the word of God, you do not have faith. Not only hearing the word of God, but hearing it on a consistent basis. You must hear the word of God over and over and over again. This (hearing the word of God) builds your faith causing you to become rooted and grounded in His word.

The word of God will be your foundation. We rarely hear God's word one time and then our faith is established. This reminds me of a couple of old phrases I have heard. "You can't knock down a wall by hitting it one time". "You can't push a cart up a hill by starting at the bottom". We knock down walls by constantly striking at it. We must constantly hit it and hit it and hit it! We should also get a running start to push that cart up the hill. We must build up the necessary momentum to cause the cart to move. Why do we need the momentum?

We have an adversary called the devil that is trying to stop you from entering into the kingdom of God system. The devil wants to hold you back and keep you from obtaining the wealth, blessings, prosperity, healing, peace and all the gifts that our salvation has earned for us. God has blessings for us that have been freely given. We have this inheritance. The earth belongs to the Lord and the devil knows it. The earth was stolen, and now we have been assigned to take it back.

This is God's desire to see his children blessed. In 3 John 1:2 'beloved, I wish above all things that thou mayest prosper and be in health, even as thy soul prospereth'. As you can tell, it is important that we press towards our inheritance. We must press toward what belongs to God. We are about our Father's business. We obtain the promises of God through consistency and obedience. The problem with pride, as it relates to faith, is that if a person attempts to do something and fails, then pride will not let them try again. Maybe they were turned down for a loan or a promotion. Pride will cause you to cave in, give up and quit. No, don't quit! Get your pride out the way, and go do it again. Never give up. Faith requires you to hear, say, and do and hear, say and do the word of God until the manifestation takes place.

In Ephesians 6:13-14 'wherefore take unto you the whole armour of God, that ye may be able to withstand in the evil day, and having done all, to stand. Stand therefore'. If a person only tries to do something once, they truly have not done all they can do to stand. They have only done all they know to do in their natural mind, but they have not done all to stand. Once you have truly done all, you will not waver, but you will stand firmly in your place. You will stand on the word of God, which is your foundation.

Will you stand alone? No, you won't. As we continue in Ephesians 6:14-17 we see what we will stand with. You are 'having your loins girt about with truth, and having on the breastplate of righteousness: and your feet shod with the preparation of the gospel of peace; above all, taking the shield of faith, wherewith ye shall be able to quench all the fiery darts of the wicked. And take the helmet of salvation, and the sword of the Spirit, which is the word of God'. Wow! We have some powerful ammunition.

We have the truth, righteousness, peace, faith, salvation, the sword of the spirit and the word of God. We can not lose. We have everything that we need. With these weapons, there is no wall that our faith can't knock down. There are no walls of containment. Once you realize why you are standing and who you are standing for and what you are standing with, you will stand, therefore. You are standing there for something. You are standing to see the word of God manifest. Shout, somebody! Ooooh weeee! Glory be to God! Thank you Jesus! Thank you Jesus! Thank you Jesus! No weapon formed against us shall prosper! We are more than conquerors! We can do all things through Christ, which strengthened us! We have the word of God on our side. All we need to do is stay focused, remain patient and continue to apply violent faith to any wall that is facing us.

Do you know what you have? Do you know the power that is contained in the word of God? We may be tested, but remember James 1:3-4 'knowing this that the trying of your faith worketh patience, but let patience have her perfect work, that ye may be perfect and entire, wanting nothing'. If our faith is tested, our patience: our ability to remain the same, standing on the word of God, will be put to work. Once patience has finished we will come out wanting nothing. We will have everything that we have been standing for. Don't give up. Don't quit. Continue to press forward.

In John 8:31-32 'if ye continue in my word, then are ye my disciples indeed; and ye shall know the truth, and the truth shall make you free'. So continue doing the work of the Lord. Continue in the word of God. As long as you continue, you will be considered a disciple or a disciplined one. Once you become disciplined about the things of God, then you will know the truth.

'Wherefore by their fruits ye shall know them' (Matthew 7:20). You will know the truth about faith and the word of God. You will know the truth about why Jesus died for our sins. You will know the truth about recognizing our enemy. You will know the truth about what the Lord has for us. This truth will propel you. This truth will motivate you. This truth will make you continue hitting the wall. You will continue pushing the cart up the hill. You will continue towards the kingdom of God. You won't give up! You won't cave in! You won't quit!

Chapter 20

Patience-waiting on the Lord...laziness

'My brethren, count it all joy when ye fall into divers temptations: knowing this that the trying of your faith worketh patience, but let patience have her perfect work, that ye may be perfect and entire, wanting nothing' (James 1:2-4). Unless you understand what it means to be patient, pride will have you waiting a long time. Pride will have you putting up with a lot of unnecessary things. Pride will make you lazy.

Let's look at this scripture. Count it all joy when you fall into temptation. This sounds like you should laugh or have fun when you have problems. I don't know about you, but it ain't funny when someone gets put out of their apartment or if someone loses their job. I don't see anything to be hilarious about. I personally don't see the joy in that situation. However, in the second part of the verse 'knowing this. You should have joy 'knowing this that the trying of your faith worketh patience'. Now, this is making better sense.

We should have joy because we know that our faith is on trial. Our faith is in the word of God. The word of God is on trial. Oh, now it is easier to have joy because I know and have faith that 'the word of God shall not return void and it will always produce' (Isaiah 55:11). I can count it all joy because I know that the word of God will always come through in the midst of my temptations.

Where does patience come in? Patience is the back up of faith. Patience is like a bodyguard to faith. Every time faith is on trial, patience will show up on the scene. Faith cannot go anywhere without patience being right beside it. Patience is what supports your faith. We must first understand the meaning of patience. Patience does not mean to put up with. Patience means to remain the same. You must have a foundation. Patience is that foundation for faith. Ask yourself, what are you being patient about?

If you still think that patience means to put up with, then why are you staying in an abusive relationship? Why are you staying broke and poor? Are you waiting for your mate to change? Are you waiting for a better job? Is that what you call patience? We have just learned that patience shows up when faith is on trial, so this is letting me know that patience has a covenant. Faith is a covenant word. Faith is based on the word of God. Since patience works when faith is on trial, then patience supports faith or patience supports the word of God.

If you are in an abusive relationship, but you say that you are being patient, is the abuse based on your own belief or on the word of God? If you are suffering on your job, but you call it patience, is your suffering based on your own belief or on the word of God? I don't mean to burst your bubble, but if your waiting or patience is not based on the word of God, then you are not truly patient. You are actually in sin. Anything that is not of faith is sin, so if your waiting is not of faith-based on the word of God, then you might want to ask yourself, who or what are you waiting on or what are you waiting for? Are you waiting for the situation to change or are you waiting for God to change the situation?

Let's look further into the word. James 1:3-4 is letting us know that the trying of your faith works, employs or puts patience to work. When your faith is on trial, patience will go to work for you. We must let patience have her perfect work. When there is perfect work, this is a clear indication to me that something has been completed. It means that you have started in faith and that you have received the end of your faith. Once patience has reached completion, you will lack nothing. If there is still lack in your life, patience has not finished working.

What has this to do with pride? Pride will compromise. Pride will change its course. The world's system of 'situation ethics' will set in. Right won't always be right or wrong won't always be wrong. It will depend on the situation. Patience will stay constant and consistently the same. Regardless of the situation or regardless of the circumstance, patience will run its course until completion.

'Ye are in need of patience, that, after ye have done the will of God, ye might receive the promise' (Hebrews 10:36). Once you have done the will of God, which is the word of God, you will obtain the promise. However, God said you still need patience. Patience has often been referred to as the twin of faith. We call faith and patience 'the power twins'. They go together, hand-in-hand. Faith, which is the word of God along with patience, which is remaining the same about your faith in the word of God, will always produce manifestation.

Do not allow pride to move you or change you. Do not allow pride to cause you to justify your reasons for not remaining the same. To me, this is laziness. This means that a person was lazy and inconsistent about changing. They conform to the world's system. They give up. Anytime people begin to justify themselves or give reasons and excuses for things they do not do, it is probably their inability to stay the same. It is their excuse to change. It is an excuse to not be patient.

I once heard an example about a surfer who demonstrated true patience. He was riding a surfboard while the wind was blowing hard. The water formed huge waves under the surfer, which almost caused him to fall. Even while the waves, winds, and waters were constantly trying to shake the surfboard and knock the rider off, the surfer kept surfing. He stayed on the surfboard. The surfer remained the same. The surfer finished the course. The surfer was patient.

We must learn to control our emotions while being patient. It sounds simple to have faith and to let patience support our faith. What about when we have faith and patience, but we see the sinner just rejoicing? We know or think they don't have faith, because faith is keeping the word of God and obeying His commandments. What do we do? Jeremiah 12:1-5 will answer that question. Jeremiah prayed to God 'righteous art thou, O Lord, when I plead with thee: yet let me talk with thee of thy judgments: Wherefore doth the way of the wicked prosper? Wherefore are all they happy that deal very treacherously'?

Jeremiah was literally saying to God that he needed to complain to Him about a few things. How come the wicked people are prospering and they seem very happy? In verse 3 Jeremiah continued complaining by saying 'but thou, O Lord knowest me: thou hast seen me, and tried mine heart toward thee: pull them out like sheep for the slaughter, and prepare them for the day of slaughter'.

Now he is saying: "what about me"? "I have been faithful. I have been patient. I have done the things you asked me to do. You know my heart. Lord, it is not fair. If I were you I would just kill all of those wicked people just like sheep going to a slaughter". Jeremiah just continued complaining. He even included the land, the herbs and the animals in his misery. He told God that they are mourning also. (It's true that misery loves company.)

God finally gave Jeremiah an answer. Now, if any person reading this book right now is tired of being patient and waiting on the Lord, listen closely to what God told Jeremiah. In verse 5 'If thou hast run with the footmen, and they have wearied thee, then how canst thou contend with horses? And if in the land of peace, wherein thou trustedst, they wearied thee, then how wilt thou do in the swelling of Jordan'. The amplified version says that the Lord rebuked Jeremiah's impatience. He literally told Jeremiah if you are tired now, then what will you do when things really get rough? If you can't keep up on foot, how can you compete with a horse?

If you get frustrated at seeing other people blessed, how are you going to feel 'if' they become millionaires? Jeremiah, where is your heart? Jeremiah, can I trust you where you are now? Will you always give up? Jeremiah, where is your patience? Why are you so worried and so concerned about the wicked? Your attention should be on God, and not on the world.

God was truly upset at how impatient Jeremiah was. 'But let him that glorieth glory in this, that he understandeth and knoweth me, that I am the Lord which exercise lovingkindness, judgment, and righteousness in the earth: for in these things I delight, saith the Lord' (Jeremiah 9:24).

Now, are any of you similar to Jeremiah? Do you get upset to look at someone else being blessed? Are you tired of waiting for God to bless you? Do you keep wondering when will it be your turn to rejoice? Listen closely. You should rejoice right now! The Lord wants you to rejoice where you are now. Count it all joy because you know that the trying of your faith will work patience. Don't allow impatience, laziness or pride to knock you off that surfboard. Don't compare yourself to anyone else. Your relationship is with God, and God will supply all of your needs. It is not your job or your responsibility to judge anyone else. You only need to judge yourself. You only need to look at yourself in the mirror, and tell the Lord, "I have patience".

I will remain the same until you bless me. I once heard some say that they were going to hang on to the Lord until He blessed them. That is the attitude we should all have. We should always be willing to wait on the Lord. God may not come when you want Him to come, but remember, He is always right on time. Your time will come. Due season always come. Let patience have her perfect work. Let patience complete her job so you will come out with everything that you were standing for.

Don't complain about your situation. When a person is not satisfied with the small blessings in his life right now, how will he appreciate it when the Lord truly blesses him? Avoid being impatient, but remain patient. Remain the same. Rebuke any type of mood swings or emotional changes. Don't be tossed like a ship by everything that you see or hear. Have faith and patience, knowing that the Lord hears your prayer and know that He will bless you with what you have prayed for. I pray peace over your life. I pray patience over your life. In the name of Jesus, Amen.

Chapter 21

Pride...the power twin of fear...conceited

People think that a person who walks in pride is very strong. They see a very confident and sturdy person. It may appear that nothing bothers them or that they are not afraid of anything. In actuality, many times it is the complete opposite. Pride is a cover-up. Pride hides from reality. Pride is like a band-aid that tries the hide its true wounds and pains.

What do I mean? A carnal minded person does not recognize his true source of power. They operate in the flesh, therefore, they are always trying to control or discipline the flesh. The problem is that the bible has made it very clear that the flesh has no power. In Matthew 26:41 the word of faith is 'to watch and pray, that ye enter not into temptation'. Why? 'The spirit is indeed willing, but the flesh is weak'.

Pride operates in the flesh, and the flesh is weak. This means that pride is also a weakness. Does this mean that a person who walks in pride is actually weak and not strong? Yes. First of all, weak people always need support. They always need someone to hold them up. This does not matter whether the support is willfully given or not, some type of support is there. When we walk up steps, they support us even though they don't move. Secondly, a weak person always has fear inside of them. "What if I fall?" Since they know that they are weak, they try to avoid confrontations that they feel will overpower them.

What would happen if they showed their weaknesses? For one, they would receive no respect from the world and its system. They would always be defeated. At this point, they have a choice. They could either appear weak, as they really are or they could appear strong and arrogant to hide the real person. (Remember, I am still talking about people who operate in the flesh and not in the spirit.)

In order not to show any signs of weakness, a person of pride will always have the band-aid on to cover-up or hide their fears and weaknesses. In 1 Peter 5:8 'Be sober, be vigilant; because your adversary the devil, as a roaring lion, walketh about, seeking whom he may devour'. Pride is as a roaring lion. Pride has a lot of 'bark' but no 'bite'. Notice also in this scripture that the devil walks around seeking whom he may devour. This is a clear indication that the devil has no power. Secondly, he cannot devour everybody. He can only devour the ones who let him.

A personal testimony: I don't believe that things 'just happen' in a person's life. Our status in life today is based on a seed that was sown in the past. The situation I was trapped in for so many years was pride. It was not until I began writing this book that I learned how to discover myself. I found out who I am and how did I become this way.

We see different types of people everyday and it seems that they all have their own unique way of thinking. Some people are nice while others are mean. Some people are giving while others are stingy. Some people will help you live while others will try to kill you.

Have you ever wondered what happened? Have you ever wondered why that person is the way that they are? It did not just happen. I strongly believe that some type of seed was sown in their life that has conformed them to be someone that they really are not. Some people may curse and then say: "that slipped out of my mouth". Some say: "well, that's just the way I am" or "I can't help it". As I stated earlier, nothing just happens.

In my personal life, I have been guilty of the same things. There were things that I did or said that were not very nice. I offended a lot of people. I hurt a lot of people. I used a lot of people. I did not understand why I did these things. For a long time, I just chose to accept the fact of that was just the way I am. I used to have nightmares about a horrifying event that happened to me when I was a young child.

I lived with my daddy all of my life. My parents separated when I was only 2 years old. (They did not get a divorce until several years later.) My mother moved back to her hometown in Dublin, GA. I was the youngest and the baby of the family. My oldest brother, Johnny Jr., who was 13 at the time, left with my mother. My oldest sister, Christine, was 12 at the time. My sister, Ileane, was 11 years old. My brother, David, was 10 and I was 2 years old. Christine moved out four years later into her own apartment. Ileane moved to Dublin with my mother. This left me, David and my daddy. David was very busy with school, baseball and friends. My daddy worked two, sometimes three jobs. Somehow, he still managed to make quality time for David and myself.

During this time, I spent a lot of time at home alone. The elementary school I attended was only 2 blocks from home. I would get home around 2:30 and would be by myself until 5:00 or sometimes later. I was only 6 years old, so I would just watch television or play in the yard.

One day two of my brother's male friends stopped by the apartment looking for him. He was not home, so they decided to wait around. (I found out later that they knew David would be home late.) They also knew my daddy was working. Needless to say, this was the longest wait of my life. They began to tickle and play catch games with me. This playtime turned into caressing, touching and eventually they began to fondle with me. The next thing I knew, my pants and underwear were pulled off and I found myself being molested. I did not know exactly what was going on at the time. All I knew was that I was in pain, and I was too scared to tell anyone. I did not know what my brother or daddy would do. I thought I would get in trouble for letting his friends in the house while nobody was at home.

Unfortunately, this event did not stop on this one day. As far as I can remember, these two boys raped me from age 6-9. (It might have been longer, but a part of my childhood has been blocked from my memory.) My whole entire life, I carried so much anger and rebellion inside of me. I was hoping that those boys who did this to me would drop dead off the face of this earth. I stopped trusting people. I did not socialize. I became isolated and remained all to myself. I wanted to open up to people, but I only let them into to my life with a limit.

However, my childhood activities continued to be normal. I was a star athlete in baseball and basketball. I played a little street football. I was raised with my father, so I still learned about the responsibilities of being a man and all that it took to provide for a household. I was an honor graduate in high school and an honor student in college. I still dated (women, of course) and I even had girlfriends. I exceeded in every job I ever had. As you can tell, the incident that happened when I was 6 did not stop me from existing on this earth.

However, that was the problem. I was only 'existing' and not 'living' my life to the fullest. I held back a lot: especially in relationships. I was very quiet because I was trying to get a feel for people. I was trying to discern and understand the type of person they were. I would listen to the things they said and I watched closely the things that they did. I was in bondage to people because I did not know what to expect or what harm they would try and cause in my life. I always seemed to be driven by my emotions instead of being directed by God.

I am telling this story as a testimony to somebody. I was raped; however, I still chose to go on with my life and ultimately, become the man that God called me to be. I refused to let a very embarrassing and shameful part of my past dictate to me how my future will be. Yes, I have thought about the ordeal I went through and I have had many nightmares. But, I thank God for blessing me with a loving and a very disciplined daddy. I thank God that I had a praying mother. Nobody knew (until now) that this happened in my life. The devil even tried to remind me of what happened. When the devil tries to remind me of any part of my past, I simply remind him of his future. Thank you Jesus!

Unfortunately, I became conceited and was walking in pride. I did not even realize it. Conceited means more than just being 'stuck up' or thinking that you are better than someone else is. It means shame and vanity. The root word of conceited is to 'conceal'. When you conceal something you hide it or cover it up. I was trying to hide and conceal this shameful event that happened in my life. In order to protect myself and to keep people from knowing about my past, I sometimes rebelled. This is why I did not socialize. I was in fear of someone uncovering something I had been trying to hide my entire life. This is pride.

Since I became born again at age 12, the Lord has guided me and directed me down the right path. I could have decided to change my sexual preference. I am sure there are many other men that could have also. I thank God for ordering my steps and for guiding my feet in the direction that He would have me to go. I yielded myself to God and allowed the Holy Spirit to come upon me. The spirit of the Lord healed my broken and wounded spirit. Instead of conforming to an incident of being raped, the Lord transformed me into a mighty man of Valor; a man of Distinction; a man of Integrity; a man of God! Just like everything else in my life, I had a choice. I was not going to sign for any package that was not in agreement with the word of God. It was delivered to my door; nevertheless, it did not mean I had to sign for it. Just because Federal Express delivers mail to your door does not mean that it belongs to you. It is not until you sign for it that you claim it.

Do not sign for any package of fear, doubt or unbelief. You sign for those packages by meditating on negative situations. You sign for the package by worrying or by speaking and confessing those thoughts. We sign for a package of fear through anger, actions, and in so many other ways. Since fear does not belong to you, do not sign for that package.

I once saw a movie about a detective who was responsible for capturing a killer after a nationwide manhunt. Little did the detective know, the criminal was possessed with an evil spirit. This spirit was only able to survive in living bodies. It could move from body to body just at the slightest touch. Once inside your body, the evil spirit would take over and eventually kill its victim.

However, the spirit was unable to enter into the detective's body. His faith and belief in God, and not in the evil spirit is what protected him. His faith created a fortress of protection around his body. He encountered a lot of grief and emotional hardships by watching this evil sprit attack and destroy friends and loved ones who were close to him. His flesh began to get weak, up to a point that led him to start back smoking and drinking to calm his nerves.

This was the perfect time for that evil spirit to attack him. The detective was ready to quit. It was at this point of weakness was the evil spirit able to enter into his body, and ultimately bring the detective to his death.

There are two things I want you to notice in this movie, in which I feel led to his destruction. First, he started back smoking cigarettes. This, returning back to sin, led him to living in the flesh. In Luke 11:24-26 it speaks of when an unclean spirit is gone out of a man and is unable to return, the spirit will come back seven times worse. This is so true. If you have made a decision to drop an unhealthy habit, DO NOT even think about starting back. It will be 7 times harder to stop again. Secondly, when the detective was living in the flesh, which is already weak, this evil spirit could do whatever it wanted to do.

What could this detective have done or used to protect himself from this evil spirit? Faith and patience. 'Now, faith is the substance of things hoped for, and the evidence of things not seen' (Hebrews 11:1). 'Faith cometh by hearing and hearing by the word of God' (Romans 10:17). Faith is believing that you have received, before you see it, however, it must be based on the word of God.

The word of God is your foundation for faith. Faith is what God needs to bring manifestation of His word into your life. How does patience fit into all this? In James 1:3 'the trying of your faith worketh patience'. When your faith is on trial or when your faith is being tested, patience is the power twin that will support your faith. The detective had faith, but lacked the patience that would sustain his faith.

Faith and patience are power twins. In Hebrews 10:36 'for ye have need of patience, that, after ye have done the will of God, ye might receive the promise'. After you have done God's will, which is the word of God or after you have faith, then what you need is patience. They go together. They cannot and should not be separated.

On the opposite side of the stick, we have the power twins of the devil: pride and fear. When a person has pride, he actually has fear. When you walk in the flesh, you can't walk by the spirit. When you walk in the flesh, you can't walk by faith. Remember that faith comes by the word of God. When you have pride, you are in the flesh. When you are in the flesh, you are in sin.

How does fear come? Remember that pride is simply one form of fear. Thus, pride and fear are the power twins of the devil. Faith and patience comes from God. Pride and fear come from the devil. Look at it this way: a car battery will provide a spark to ignite the alternator. The alternator of the car keeps the car running. Faith is the spark that ignites patience, while pride is the spark that ignites fear. Patience keeps the word of God running while fear keeps the word of the devil running. It is your choice. Will you choose faith and patience or pride and fear?

Chapter 22

Hasten to His love....FREEDOM

In Romans 12:3 'for I say, through the grace given unto me, to every man that is among you, not to think of himself more highly than he ought to think; but to think soberly, according as God hath dealt to every man the measure of faith'. In the amplified bible 'for by grace (unmerited favor of God) given to me I warn everyone among you not to estimate and think of himself more highly than he ought (not to have an exaggerated opinion of his own importance), but to rate his ability with sober judgement, each according to the degree of faith apportioned by God to him'. In other words, drop your pride.

The unmerited favor of God was sent through David to warn everyone about pride. This lets me know that pride is a very serious issue with God. Pride is just as serious as a tornado, earthquake or a hurricane. When one of these 'natural disasters' was about to take place, the weather stations issued warnings to people everywhere. They know the destructive power that a tornado or hurricane can produce. They have sophisticated and high technical devices and equipment to detect a storm ahead of time.

The grace of God is the equipment used to detect the storms of pride in our lives. Pride is one of the most destructive forces that can destroy any person's life. Pride begins like a soft breeze but ends in a tornado. How does it begin? It begins with "I". It begins when a person starts to 'estimate and think of himself more highly'. People estimate or guess when they do not know the answer, so they create one that will only serve the purpose for that time. This is called assumption, which to me, is the lowest form of knowledge.

If you are the type of person who feels they do not have an identity or if they don't really know who they are, I have a solution. Examine yourself. Take a look in the mirror and ask yourself "why do I feel this way"? Continue asking yourself why until you cannot formulate any more answers.

Next, think about your past, your childhood, your parents and friends. Are there any pains or bad experiences that have happened to you in which you have not let go of? Have you learned how to forgive and to forget? Remember that you cannot go forward by holding on to the past.

Also, ask questions about your ancestors. What were your great grandparents like? What were their religious beliefs? After you have gone back as far as you can go, then you are preparing yourself to go forward.

The only reason I want you to examine yourself, your past, your childhood and your ancestors is so you can destroy any bad seeds that may be in you or your family. You may be the victim of a generational curse that is getting ready to be broken TODAY!

In the last chapter we just read, I shared with you a horrible event that happened to me which literally dictated my life for over 20 years. I never knew the danger and affect that holding grudges and anger inside of me could have on my life.

This incident took me through years of estimating, guessing and trying to figure out who I was. I used alcohol, friends, family, strangers, women, sports, isolation, clubs, music and anything else I could think of as an escape. I needed something that would give me peace in this world. I was in total search of myself.

However, it was not until I found God that I found myself. The reason I could not find God was because I was looking in the wrong place. I was looking for God in the flesh instead of in the spirit. Once I found God, I began to recognize who I was. I stopped guessing and trying to figure things out. God is a spirit, and we are made in the image of God, therefore, we are spirit beings.

Now, I am getting excited. I am made in the image of God! Wow! This gives me joy knowing where I truly come from. 'The joy of the Lord is my strength' (Nehemiah 8:10). The joy of knowing who I am in Christ is my strength. The joy of knowing what the Lord has done for me and for who He is in my life is my strength. This is my joy. The joy of the Lord! I have great joy knowing that my family history goes back to God. Somewhere along the lines, things may have gotten distorted and sidetracked. My family may have taken the wrong turn. However, I thank God for ordering my steps and for getting me back on track in order to break any generational curse over my family.

I know who I am now. I am the child of a King. My daddy (God) created this world. I have no need to look outside of the family for happiness anymore. All I have to do is look inside of myself. My spirit is who I am. There is no need to guess or estimate. Don't allow pride to have you focused on the world to find out who you are. Confess Psalm 51:10

'create in me a clean heart, O God; and renew a right spirit within me'. The real you is on the inside.

Pride will have you looking everywhere for acceptance. Pride will blind you by getting your attention off your spirit and focusing on your flesh. If a person does not know who they are, more than likely they will become someone that is not the real them.

Now, going back to Romans 12:3, this is why God warns us not to estimate who we are, but to know who we are. Regardless of what anybody else thinks, you should know who you are. You are made in the image of God. If you don't know who you are, the next thing that will happen is that you will begin to exaggerate your estimation of yourself. You will have an 'exaggerated opinion of your own importance'. This can be either arrogance or self-pity. As you can tell, pride can be exalting yourself higher or lower than you really are.

An arrogant person will think that they are responsible for their success. They feel that nobody can do a job better than they can. They feel that help is not needed from anyone. They will not want to apologize, repent or admit any faults, mistakes or imperfections. They feel that all ideas, concepts and insights come from their own intellect. It is very hard for them to receive advice since they think they know it all anyway. They can be very rebellious and controlling. They give acknowledgment to their own mind for the brilliance that they display. They must always maintain a successful image. They must always appear to people like they 'got it going on'.

Arrogance looks in the mirror and only see "I", "me", "my" and "mine" as their source for success. Arrogance looks at everyone else and only see "you", "your", "they" and "them" as the source for failure. A person of pride always sees something or someone else as the problem.

They make judgements based only on what they can see with their 'natural' eyes. They either exalt themselves or condemn others because of actions and situations that are happening. They believe in situation ethics which means 'right isn't always right and wrong isn't always wrong, it just depends on the situation'. They rarely walk in integrity.

Now, on the self-pity side, you have a person that is not single. This is an individual that feels they need someone else to make them feel complete. They rarely enjoy being alone. They sometimes can be easily offended. Offense is mainly due to a lack of confidence in one's own lives. This type of person will believe everything they hear because they don't have a solid foundation of what they consider the truth to be.

In Ephesians 4:14 'that we henceforth be no more children, tossed to and fro, and carried about with every wind of doctrine, by the sleight of men, and cunning craftiness, whereby they lie in wait to deceive'. When they have an idea, a lot of times they need reassurance or confirmation from several people. They always see someone else as a threat and not as a challenge. It is almost like they think that someone else is 'out to get them' or to hurt them. This person may try to 'fit in' or get along with everyone in order to feel accepted, liked or appreciated. They can have a very low self-esteem, which more than likely, originated from a bad seed in the past. Maybe they were called ugly names as a child, which placed a stain on their appearance for many years.

However, whether a person exalts himself higher or lower than he is, this is pride. The bible calls this an 'exaggerated opinion of his own importance'. It is time for you to grow up. In 1 Corinthians 13:11 'when I was a child, I spake as a child, I understood as a child, I thought as a child: but when I became a man, I put away childish things'.

The next stage of pride is to 'rate his ability with sober judgment' or to think soberly. This is when the devil is trying to totally confuse you. The devil will begin to use one of his most favorite tricks. He will have you thinking that the word of God will not work. This is the biggest fear to any Christian believer.

If the devil can get you to think that your tithe will not produce a harvest, that your sowing will be in vain or that you are wasting your time in any area of your life, then he can control your body. Your body basically acts out on what goes through your mind. The mind is the only place the devil can attack you. He tries to get your mind on the problem. We never feel any type of physical pain until our mind is thinking about it. He tries to conform your mind into prideful thinking.

It is at this level of pride when a person begins to 'second guess' himself. They get to a point where they don't really know what to do or what decisions to make. When a person is not 'sober' then they are 'drunk'. A person that is intoxicated does not think with a sound mind. He does not think straight. A lot of quick, rash and emotional decisions are made. The only solution to a renewed mind is a renewed spirit. When your spirit is in line with the perfect will of God, your mind will think on the perfect will of God, thus, your body will line up with the perfect will of God.

Finally, we must realize that 'God hath dealt to every man the measure of faith' or 'the degree of faith apportioned to him'. What does this mean? It means that God is not a respecter of person. It means that God has given everyone the exact same measure of faith. It is up to the individual as to how and when they use that faith. "You mean to tell me that I was given the same measure of faith as my pastor"? Yes. The only difference is that your pastor made a decision to apply his faith. He tapped into the wisdom of God.

Faith is the word of God. 'The word of God is incorruptible seed' (1 Peter 1:23) or seed that will always produce and seed that cannot be destroyed. God's word will never return to Him void or without producing. God's word will accomplish everything that it was sent forth to accomplish. People don't realize that it takes the same amount of faith to move a mountain as it does to move a rock. It takes the same amount of faith to have joy as it does to remain sad. It takes the same amount of faith to become rich as it does to be poor.

Pride will not let a person get to this stage of faith. Pride will not even let you know that this level of faith exists. Pride will not let you know that this right to have a measure of faith belongs to you. People are destroyed because of a lack of knowledge. There are people today still walking with a slave mentality. If a person does not know they have a right to do certain things, most likely, they won't take advantage of it. They don't realize that faith is a gift from God.

'The gifts and calling of God are without repentance' (Romans 11:29). This means that every gift God gives you will never be taken back. God never changes His mind about a gift He has given. It is not His fault if we lose our gifts. Hasten to the love of God. Stop, look and listen. Hearken to His word. Hear, obey and do the word of God.

Epilogue

Coming soon—*Pride II…the root to destruction–the spirit of pride.* A proud look (*the spirit* that makes one overestimate himself and underestimate others) Proverbs 6:17 Amplified. In this exciting book, you will learn how to recognize your true enemies and reveal the 'root to the fruit'. Pride is more than an unbalanced emotion, but pride is an evil spirit. *Pride II…the root to destruction–the spirit of pride* is a shocking, eye-opening experience into the reality and dangers of a deadly, inward disease that has infected and destroyed the lives of billions of people.

You will learn how to bind the spiritual forces of pride by applying violent faith with God's word. We are in a spiritual warfare so let's get prepared for this spiritual battle!

I once had a dream of a very beautiful mansion. The doorknobs were trimmed in gold; the floors were made of glass; diamond chandeliers were hanging from the ceilings of each room. This mansion was absolutely beautiful. As I continued to stare at this magnificent and priceless treasure, the scene begins to change. I started to notice tiny particles of dust falling in the air. Next, while I was looking at the floor, I noticed that the view beneath the home was showing tiny, unknown particles of some sort. The view is now getting clearer in which I am able to see the dirt, bricks and pipes underneath this mansion. A lot of dirty, muddy, sewer water is flowing in huge masses. You can also see the remains of dead rodents being eaten by their survivors. All of a sudden, I awake from this dream in a cold sweat.

The Lord spoke to my spirit and said that this is how pride looks from a heavenly view. The outward appearance may look like a beautiful mansion, but underneath, the true infected spirit reveals the root of the matter. *Pride II...the root to destruction–the spirit of pride.*

Conclusions

As I close this chapter of my life, I decree and declare that everybody, who reads the words that God has placed in my spirit, is blessed. You are now FREE! You are free from pride! You are free from the devil! You are free from any generational curses! You are free from condemnation! You are free from sin! You are FREE! You are FREE! You are FREE! Shout somebody! I am FREE! I am FREE! I am FREE! I am a new creature in Christ! I am free from the past! Old things in my life have been passed away and all things in my life are new! Today is the very first day of the rest of my life! I have wronged no man! I have a clean heart and a renewed spirit! I have the mind of Christ! I can do all things through Christ, which strengthened me!

'Finally, my brethren, be strong in the Lord, and in the power of his might. Put on the whole armour of God, that ye may be able to stand against the wiles of the devil. For we wrestle not against flesh and blood, but against principalities, against powers, against the rulers of the darkness of this world, against spiritual wickedness in high places. Wherefore take unto you the whole armour of God, that ye may be able to withstand in the evil day, and having done all, to stand. Stand therefore, having your loins girt about with truth, and having on the breastplate of righteousness; And your feet shod with the preparation of peace; Above all, taking the shield of faith, wherewith ye shall be able to quench all the fiery darts of the wicked. And take the helmet of salvation, and the sword of the Spirit, which is the word of God: Praying always with all prayer and supplication in the Spirit, and watching thereunto with all perseverance and supplication for all saints; And for me, that utterance may be given unto me, that I may open my mouth boldly, to make known the mystery of the gospel, For which I am an ambassador in bonds: that therein I may speak boldly, as I ought to speak' (Ephesians 6:10-20).

'I have fought a good fight, I have finished my course, I have kept the faith. And they overcame him by the blood of the Lamb, and by the word of their testimony. As it written, For thy sake we are killed all the daylong; we are accounted as sheep for the slaughter. Nay, in all these things we are more than conquerors through him that loved us. For I am persuaded that neither death, nor life, nor angels, nor principalities, nor powers, nor things present, nor things to come, Nor height, nor depth, nor any other creature, shall be able to separate us from the love of God, which is in Christ Jesus our Lord' (2 Timothy 4:7; Revelations 12:11; Romans 8:36-39).

I seal this book with the anointing of God. I seal this book with the Holy Spirit. In the name of Jesus Christ I pray. Amen.

Always remember that God is good, and His word declares that if we confess our faults He is faithful to forgive us and to cleanse us from all unrighteousness. Simply, repeat this prayer with me:

Father God, I declare that nobody but Jesus Christ sits on the throne on my life, and because He is in my life I have righteousness, peace and joy in the Holy Ghost. I repent for all of my sins: committed or omitted, known or unknown, or thought about or spoken. I ask you to forgive me for any form of pride that may have been in my life. I submit myself to you and I resist the devil and any evil work. The devil and anything of him must flee from my life. My heart is pure, and I walk in honesty, truth and integrity because I submit my life to you. Thank you for forgiving me, and giving me favor to make a change in my life forever. In Jesus name I pray. Amen.

SALVATION

I recognize and admit that I am a sinner. I am a sinner through inheritance of Adam and Eve because I was born in sin. I repent of my sins and ask you to forgive me. I now have a change of heart, a change of mind, and a change of direction. I will turn away from sin and submit to God. I confess with my mouth and I believe in my heart that God raised Jesus from the dead for me. I declare that I am now saved and my life has been redeemed from destruction. I make a decision now to meditate, study and obey God's word and to keep His commandments forever. In Jesus name. Amen.

About the Author

Ronnie J. Wells graduated from Griffin High School in Griffin, Georgia in 1986. He also graduated from Branell Business College in College Park, Georgia. He is the youngest of 5 children born to the late Johnny Wells, Sr. and Mrs. Annie Chambers Wells, who currently reside in Dublin, Georgia. He attended Middle Georgia Jr. College with hopes of becoming a professional basketball player.

Being raised in an under-developed area in Griffin allowed him to see the realization of crime and punishment at an early age. Ronnie has enjoyed writing all of his life and has a collection of short stories and motivational literature. *Pride…the root to destruction* was inspired through many personal experiences in his life that he placed on scrap paper and note pads while riding on the trains and buses in the suburbs of Metro Atlanta, Georgia.

He is also a former President and Area Governor of ToastMasters International, which is a speech writing and public speaking training program. Ronnie is a faithful member of World Changers Church International in College Park, Georgia, as well as a servant of the Lord for various outreach ministries, which includes Lee Haney's Harvest House, WCCI Barrier Breakers Men's Ministry and Danny Finkley Outreach Ministries.

Currently, Ronnie and his wife Conchata live in southeast Atlanta with children Zakarius, Breana, Camara, Jeremy and Ronni-Christina.